ON DIFFICULTY AND OTHER ESSAYS

By the same author
After Babel (1975)

GEORGE STEINER, 1929 –

On Difficulty

and Other Essays

New York and Oxford

OXFORD UNIVERSITY PRESS

1978

Library of Congress Catalogue Card Number: 78-40280

Printed in the United States of America

For

Donald and Lois MacKinnon

Contents

Preface

Administrative and bureaucratic practice has disseminated the terms 'working papers' or, notably in American idiom, 'position papers'. These terms could be useful in defining a certain stage and style of intellectual argument. A 'working' or a 'position' paper puts forward a point of view, an analysis, a proposal, in a form which may be comprehensive and assertive. It seeks to clarify the 'state of the art' at some crucial point of difficulty or at a juncture from which alternative directions can be mapped. But its comprehension and assertiveness are explicitly provisional. They aim at an interim status. They solicit correction, modification, and that collaborative disagreement on which the hopes of rational discourse depend. A 'working paper', a 'position paper', is one which intends to elicit from those to whom it is addressed a deepening rejoinder and continuation.

The essays in this collection are composed entirely in this vein. Within the general field of the understanding of language, of the more recent philosophic and linguistic ways of approaching the meaning of meaning, they try to set out certain 'frontier' topics. The word 'frontier' has two relevant senses. The topics discussed are at the forward edge of current thought and scholarship. They are not yet clearly or fully understood. And what needs to be done is to formulate questions about them in as sharp and fruitful a way as possible. Thus, there are papers in this book on the relations between erotic sensibility and linguistic conventions as they are reflected or obscured in literature, and on the virtually unexplored subject of the history and formal structure of inward speech, of the language-stream we direct towards ourselves. 'Frontier' also aims to suggest that these essays locate their analyses and examples at those points where different disciplines and areas of study meet. The essay on difficulty deals with considerations which are simultaneously philosophical and literary. The initial comment on the current status of texts touches on political and sociological motifs. In several of these papers, there are attempts to clarify somewhat the intricate overlaps between linguistics, poetics and techniques of decipherment developed in psychoanalysis.

Though these papers have, with one exception, been produced over a rather concentrated period, and though they stem closely from problems examined and models set out in *After Babel* (1975), it would be idle to claim for them any rigorous unity. But it may well be that two themes give coherence to what are different and particular presentations. The first theme is that of privacy, of the altering weight of energy and of emphasis as between the inner and the outer, the voiced and the silent, the public and the private sectors of personality and speech. Could it be that vital resources of inwardness, of disciplined remembrance, of meditative clarity, fundamental to a classical culture, are being eroded by new ideals of extrovert and total utterance? The second theme is that of the changing technical, psychological and social status of the act of reading. Are there ways in which current practices of and attitudes towards the written word are making it more difficult for us to read with natural immediacy and pleasure the works, the structures of language, on which our literacy has been founded? The essay on reading Dante now seeks to make this inquiry concrete, and the closing paper is a speculation — nothing more — on what might be some of the forms of transition towards new media of articulate imagination. Obviously, these two themes and the underlying consideration of a possible dispersal of established values, will touch at many points.

It is my hope that these discussions will interest the general reader as well as the specialist who, necessarily, prefers to work within a single technical domain. To ask larger questions is to risk getting things wrong. Not to ask them at all is to constrain the life of understanding to fragments of reciprocal irony or isolation. Such constraint now marks considerable areas of political and intellectual discussion, making dissent sterile instead of productive and humane. Why this should be the case and what, if anything, we can do about it is, I imagine, the central issue of these essays, as it has been of almost everything I have written.

GS
Geneva
January 1978

ON DIFFICULTY AND OTHER ESSAYS

1

Text and Context

1976

If there is currently a debate on 'culture' — as distinct from a merely formal academic-journalistic rhetoric or rhetorical gossip — it involves, it must, where it is honestly pursued, involve the nature of 'texts'. It must bear, at crucial points of definition and dissent, on the question of the status of the 'text' and of our relations to it. One of the obvious difficulties is that this question entails the sort of understanding of the underlying realities of culture, of the conditions of co-existence between 'culture' and other, competing models of social cohesion or ideals, which an analysis of our relations to 'texts' is meant to elucidate. In other words: the argument runs a constant risk of circularity. Determine your 'reading' of culture in order to locate, to ascertain in what measure there persists, a 'culture of reading'. But hermeneutics — the disciplined understanding of understanding — instructs us that such circularity, albeit by no means comfortable or immune from logical attack, is an inevitable, perhaps necessary attribute of any discourse, of any articulate commentary whose object is itself 'textual'.

The problem is not only one of circularity. To 'think through' the question, the situation (*penser la situation*) of 'the text' in our contemporary culture, is to engage in a whole number of theoretic and pragmatic fields whose own limits or methodological integrity, whose own implication of textual authority or repudiation of the canonic, are unclear. A consideration of the convention of reading in this or that locale and section of the community, of the techniques of conservation, reproduction, diffusion, deletion or, indeed,

suppression which determine the literal availability of texts —
these topics are, broadly speaking, sociological. That the process of comprehension, the act of understanding and response — which crude formula presumably covers an
immensely complex dynamic or dialectic of impulse and
ordering — is also *social*, that there is a social-economic-
political matrix of reading as there is of the book as a
material fact, is a recognition which emerges with Dilthey
and is then refined by Walter Benjamin. If there is a sociology
of the text and of our relations to the text, there is also, of
course, a psychology. The structures of attention, of memora-
tion, of verbalization in and through which the act of reading
takes place, are neither uniform nor stable. Modern art-
historians have taught us a good deal about the developing
history of visual, tactile perception, about the essential
'historicity' of the eye in regard to perspective, volume, distortion and codes of chromatic or gestural meaning. The
psychological configurations of reading, the reflexes of
awareness which organize our 'ingestion' (Ben Jonson's term)
of the text are, certainly, no less temporal, no less the
product of the intricate congruence of innate and environ-
mental options. Here, as in the history of art or of musical
form, the 'simplest' cognitive moment involves processes,
interactive and in constant motion, which extend from the
neuro-physiological at one end to the most unstable, difficult
to document elements of fashion, social contingence, local
accident at the other. St. Augustine's often-cited observation that his teacher was the first man he knew capable of
reading without moving his lips, Erasmus's occasional testimony as to the effect of print on the very immediacies of
thought, the work of Robert Escarpit in France on the
current conditions of reading at different points and age-
levels in a mass-consumer society, are among the few markers
we have. The sociology, the psychology (or, at a fundamental

remove, neuro-physiology), the social-psychology — the awkwardness, the overlap in our rubrics being themselves symptomatic — of reading, of our relations to texts, remain rudimentary. Thus we have histories of books, of paper, of inks and typography, but none of reading.

I have been using the words 'reading' and 'text' as if the concordance between them were almost tautological. We know that it is nothing of the kind. The overwhelming proportion of reading — statistically, demographically, over any given stretch of time — has little to do with 'texts' as the argument I am pursuing defines them, a definition present to, functional in our sensibility (given an academic locale) even before it is formally phrased. Most acts of reading, shall we say ninety-five per cent simply to exemplify the grossness of evidence, occur in a context (note the opaque yet vital contiguities of 'text' and 'context'), are objectivized with regard to ends, which can only be called ephemeral, utilitarian, mechanical, nearly somnambular. Forests pass into pulp in an enactment, at once palpable and allegoric, of programmatic oblivion. Millions of tons of paper, print, ink pass through a daily cycle of instant obsolescence. This construct of insignificance, with its paradoxically contrastive technical virtuosity and economic-political consequence, reaches far or, to allow the vertical presumption, 'high' into the enterprise of letters. Many books which had aspired to the 'textual' are, in fact, pulp, the categorization being either immediate (in the United States in particular, many novels are remaindered within weeks of their first publication) or following on a certain lapse of time and revaluation. The serious newspaper or magazine article knows a problematic 'half-life'. Like 'happenings' of which it is often a generative element, it carries within it mechanisms of auto-destruction whose force is often proportionate to the urgency, to the honesty of the statement. And the article, editorial, reportage may become 'textual', via a subtle modulation of setting, when the historian returns to it as a primary source.

Even explicit trivia, moreover, press powerfully on the general and complex shapes of reading, in one's personal inventory of time and feeling and in that of the society as a whole. The temptation of universality, of echo prolonged to the outmost reaches of 'the public', exercises all but the most arcane, the most deliberately *minoritaires* among writers. The examples or exemplary myths of writers at once 'great' by any criteria of seriousness, of imaginative nerve, of stylistic autonomy *and* immensely popular — a Dickens, a Balzac, a Tolstoy — haunt literature and the critical argument on the status of literature. We apprehend vaguely, there having been so little substantive work in the field since Q.D.Leavis's pioneering *Fiction and the Reading Public*, that the history of the ephemeral, that the question of reading as mass-entertainment, cannot be divorced from that of 'texts', that the 'lower', being statistically and in terms of social attitudes so much the more ubiquitous, presses on, penetrates into the 'higher' and is, in turn, influenced by it. Trash will often mirror excellence, setting up 'resonance' effects, reciprocal redefinitions which are genuinely dialectical, and in certain genres — narrative verse, melodrama, the Gothic novel, prose fiction almost in its entirety — the line between the two is always unstable. Our definition of the class of texts and of the location of this class in the overall structure of literacy will, therefore, be in some degree an abstraction, a hypo-statization inherently suspect and defensible only if it is, at every point, kept vulnerable to the inroads of altering fact.

And yet, at some level of provisional trust, we do know, we must know what we mean by discriminating between 'print' and 'text', between 'books' as a pragmatic counter and 'the book' as the executive medium of 'the textual'. Such knowledge, such rational intuition, draws on key correlatives of disinterestedness, of semantic level, of the contract of expectation and response as negotiated, usually unconsciously, between writer and reader (or reader yet to be *because* the writing is there). The precise determination of these correlatives would be both a history of culture and of serious reading. It might lead to a short-hand recognition or working hypothesis: a 'text' is generated where the reader is one who rationally conceives of himself as writing a 'text' comparable in stature, in degree of demand, to that which he is reading. To read essentially is to entertain with the writer's text a relationship at once recreative and rival. It is a supremely active, collaborative yet also agonistic affinity whose logical, if not actual, fulfillment is an 'answering text'.

Does such reading have any natural place in our present psychological and social modes? How does it relate to the notion of culture (where is 'text' in context?)?

One answer, at least, is obvious, though the political climate in which we have conducted our lives over the past thirty years has obscured it. Marxism-Leninism and the ideological idiom professed in communist societies are 'bookish' to the root. The scheme of origins, authority and continuum in force in the Marxist world derives its sense of identity and its daily practices of validation or exclusion from a canon of texts. It is the reading of these texts — exegetic, Talmudic, disputative to an almost pathological degree of semantic scruple and interpretative nicety — which constitutes the presiding dynamic in Marxist education and in the attempts, inherently ambiguous as are all attempts to 'move forward' from sacred texts, to make of Marxism an unfolding, predictive reality-principle. The critique, 'textual' in the deepest sense, of the ancient empiricists, of Hegel and of Feuerbach, impels Marx's own writings. The critique of alternative texts — Proudhon, Dühring, Ernst Mach, Bogdanov — is the fundamental occasion and performative genre of the great body of theoretical writing from Marx and Engels down to Lenin's *Empirio-Criticism* and *Philosophical Notebooks*. The primary reflex in Marxist feeling and political-social application is that of citation, of re-reading. The ideology is made ongoing and applicable to novel circumstance by virtue of textual re-interpretation, a process which, itself, engenders a new corpus of texts ('new' yet teleologically latent in the canon). It is incumbent in the function of supreme power, or was until very lately, that the holder contribute substantial theoretic work. Stalin's writings on party principles or during the polemics on linguistics in the 1950s are, in this respect, less contemptible than one's knowledge of the man would have led one to hope. He also was a collator, close reader and 'textualist' whose *odium philologicum* inspired a massive body of written work.

As Loren R. Graham has shown in his seminal study of *Science and Philosophy in the Soviet Union*, the result is a subtlety and self-sustaining intensity of debate which permeates Soviet intellectual life and which, to an extent largely unregistered in the West, has survived the recurrent terrors. But this essential bookishness goes much beyond ideology and schooling. If it is the medium of power and official discourse, it is, no less, that of opposition. The antecedents here are plainly pre-Bolshevik; they lie in the very fabric of suppression which defines Russian history as a whole. But whatever the source, the effect is clear: the subversive poem, novel, satirical comedy, underground ballad has always been, is, will continue to be, the primary act of insurgence. Even where it has reached the public surface, through the censor's oversight, from abroad, or in brief spells of bureaucratic condescension, Russian literature, from Pushkin and Turgenev to Pasternak and Solzhenitsyn, has always been *samizdat*. The cost in personal suffering, in the eradication of personal talent, has been vast; nothing can make up for the psychological hounding to destruction of a Gogol, for the liquidation of a Mandelstam. But the paradoxical gain has also been eminent. No society reads more vehemently, to none is the writer a more indispensable presence. No oppression has ever felt more threatened by the poet's image, none has ever paid to the written word, to the text, the tribute of a more savage vigilance. Czarism and Stalinism are incommensurable structures of obscurantism and chastisement, yet structures proportionately vulnerable to, shaken by, the adverse text. The cases of Tolstoy, of Pasternak, of Solzhenitsyn show that the balance of power between the state and the writer's single voice (between context and text) is, at some level, very nearly equal. What Western regime flinches at a poem?

Below the plane of political terror and challenge, Russian existence, together with that of much of eastern Europe, is 'bookish', is penetrated by literate values. The classics are printed in mountainous editions, snapped up and read. A very considerable body of poetry, and of new poetry, is known by heart, is passed from mouth to mouth (oral traditions mesh at this point with political necessity). Arguments on literature, on the condition of the novel, on drama, are not academic or at the specialized margin of the life of feeling. They are conducted and felt to be at the core. The consequences are far too pervasive and ambiguous to be summed up readily. But in respect of humane necessity, of philosophic stature, of sheer dimension, the comparison between Western literatures after, say, Thomas Mann, with that produced in, *underneath* the Soviet Union from Blok and Mandelstam to the present is, to say the least, unsettling.

The resort to the 'canonic' via quotation, commentary, knowledge by heart and *mimesis*, was, of course, the backbone of Western literacy, of the cultures of civility which were in effective control in the West from the late Middle Ages until the recent crises of the old order. The scriptural-patristic canon on the one hand, the Greek-Latin on the other, and the perpetual interplay, critical and conjunctive, between the Hebraic and the Hellenic lineage of texts, very largely generated and organized the shapes of western public speech and personal identity among the educated. Ovid's or Horace's tags on the immortality of the major text, tags themselves reproductive of high common-places in Homer and Pindar, became the talismanic cliché of Christian-classical education and self-fulfillment. They culminate, with perfect logic, in Napoleon's claim that he would rather have written *Werther* than won his battles and in Mallarmé's proposition that the aim of the universe is the creation of *le Livre* (the 'text of texts' so integral, so comprehensive of truth and ontological form, that it subsumes, negates all 'context').

That this hierarchy of values is now eroded, that the shared habits of biblical-classical reference, of articulate formality, of 'order and degree' both emblematic and expressly rhetorical on which the intellectual-social-political architecture of the Renaissance, the Enlightenment and the nineteenth century were built, is now largely in ruins, that the very invocation of such values is a piece of élitist nostalgia — these are banalities of current debate. Knowledge by heart of the 'texts' has been done away with by the organised amnesia which now pervades schooling. The familiarity with scripture, the Book of Common Prayer, with the great current of liturgical allusion and ritual routine, which is presumptive in the speech and inference of English literature from Chaucer to Auden, is largely dissipated. Like the fabric of classical reference, citation, pastiche, parody, imitation, within which English poetry developed from Caxton's Ovid to T.S.Eliot's *Sweeney Among the Nightingales*, biblical literacy is passing quickly into the deep-freeze of academic-ism. The 'text' is receding from immediacy, from vital personal recognition on stilts of foot-notes, ever more rudimentary, ever more unashamed in their conveyance of information which was once the alphabet of reading. Greek and Latin are, finally, becoming 'dead tongues'. Less visible but equally significant is the death within our language, within our ready apprehension of the language, of that central historicity, density of cross-reference, felt syntactic and semantic elaboration which were, to be sure, related to atticism and latinity, but which also had their own prodigal life. The archival energies of Joyce, of Eliot, of Pound, the many-layered structures of allusion which characterize their work, are a ceremony of mourning for resources once naturally accessible to writer and reader in the contract of culture.

The causes of this change have been canvassed interminably. They are too manifold, we are too nearly implicated in them, to allow of any single, confident diagnosis. The breakdown of the old frameworks of 'high culture' or 'high literacy' is quite obviously inseparable from the partial collapse of those hierarchies of aristocratic, mandarin or bourgeois power-principles which a high culture embodies, articulates and transmits. The partial destruction of the old order through world wars and inflation, the transfer of material energies to various modes of populism and 'mass culture' (a term which may be inherently self-contradictory) were attended by a concomitant decay in both the systematic and external presence of the 'transcendent' — whether theological or aesthetic-philosophical. There are sovereign literacies in the sciences; indeed, these engage the most scrupulous, adventurous of our mental means and have done so, very likely, for at least a century. But such literacies are not language-centred, they are not oriented towards the 'text'. There are other causes or symptoms of the crisis of 'textuality' or 'logocentrism' (to use a peculiarly rebarbative but illuminating word) which belong, distinctly, to the socio-logical and psychological domain. The economics, the physical environment of daily existence, particularly in the most technologically-advanced communities in the West, does not make for the personal acquisition of libraries in the old manner. The pace of being, the surrounding noise-levels, the competitive stimulus of alternative media of information and entertainment (a plurality notably lacking in the Soviet Union), militate against the compacted privacy, the invest-ments of silence, required by serious reading. Self-bestowal on a text, the vertigo of attention which bends the scholar's back and blears the eye, is a posture simultaneously sacrifi-cial and stringently selfish. It feeds on a stillness, on a sanc-tuary of egotistical space, which exclude even those closest to one. Today's ideals of familial co-existence, of genera-tional amity, of neighbourliness are participatory, collective, non-dismissive. Music, performed or listened to, meets these social-emotive needs and aims as reading does not. The new humanistic literacies, where we can fairly make them out, are musical, not textual. Eloquence is suspect, formal speech is palsied with the lies, political, theological, moral, which it articulated and adorned. The honest man sings or mumbles.

Reactions to this metamorphosis of values differ as widely as do the analyses of cause. At one end of the spectrum there is celebration. Away with the malodorous dead. Make all things new. Books have too long done our thinking, our seeing, our very living for us, interposing a secondhand authority between ourselves and the innocence of immediate being. Down with museums, those mortuaries of imposed glory. Let art flower in the street and vanish at the next rain, only to be renewed in a constant simulacrum of Eden. Away with the proscenium arch; let the audience be part of, be inwoven in the play. To the wall with conductors and the tyranny of scores; a man must do, must play his own thing. (That all these slogans and gestures of millenarian bliss begin with Dada, at the exact moment of the most lunatic slaughter on the western front, is, of course, no accident. The sleep of reason does not only release nightmares; it animates the ancient dreams of total renewal, of prelapsarian spontaneity.) At the opposite pole there is desolation, more or less stoic.

Saying this, I have in mind a group of arguments on the instrumentality of reading, on the relations of the act of reading to the possibilities of culture and society, in short: a set of 'texts on texts'. Though written from differing perspectives and, partly at least, in mutual unawareness, these writings will, with time, be seen to form a significant cluster and will, I believe, assume growing importance. They include the early sections of Charles Péguy's *Dialogue de l'histoire et de l'âme païenne* of 1909; Heidegger's articles on Hölderlin composed, mainly, during the 1940s and the two essays on Nietzsche's 'Death of God' and on a saying by Anaximander, published in *Holzwege* in 1950; Philip Rieff's *Fellow Teachers*, which first appeared in 1972; and the consideration on the role of the classics in American education and society which Donald Carne-Ross enunciated in *Arion* in 1973. The discriminations to be made between these texts, and the definition of their profound, underlying concordance would need careful study. But central to each is a conception of literacy, of literacy enacted in regard to a canonic 'textuality' of the kind expressed by Péguy (quotation from whom is, given the seamless, pulsing mechanics of his prose, always arbitrary and unsatisfactory):

il ne faudrait jamais cesser d'être des *lecteurs*; des lecteurs purs, qui lisent pour lire, non pour s'instruire, non pour travailler . . . qui d'une part sachent lire et d'autre part qui veuillent lire, qui enfin tout uniment pour la voir et la recevoir, qui lisent une oeuvre tout uniment pour la lire et la recevoir, pour s'en alimenter, pour s'en nourrir, comme d'un aliment precieux, pour s'en faire croître, pour s'en faire valoir, intérieurement, organiquement, nullement pour *travailler avec*, pour s'en faire valoir, socialement, dans le siècle; des hommes aussi, des hommes enfin qui sachent lire, et ce que c'est que lire, c'est à dire que c'est *entrer dans*.

Each of these diagnosticians of our estate share Péguy's definition of what a full act of reading signifies:

Une lecture bien faite, une lecture honnête, une lecture simple, enfin, une lecture bien lue est comme une fleur, comme un fruit venu d'une fleur . . . la représentation que nous nous donnons d'un texte est comme la représentation que l'on nous donne d'une oeuvre dramatique (et aussi que nous nous donnons) . . . elle n'est pas moins que le vrai, que le véritable et même et surtout que le réel achèvement du texte, que le réel achèvement de l'oeuvre; comme un couronnement; comme une grâce particulière et coronale . . . comme une atteinte; comme une nourriture et un complément et un complément de nourriture; comme une sorte de complètement de nourriture; comme une sorte de complètement d'alimentation et ensemble d'opération. *La simple lecture est l'acte commun, l'opération commune du lisant et du lu,* de l'auteur et du lecteur, de l'oeuvre et du lecteur, du texte et du lecteur.

They would, finally, concur in Péguy's conviction that such reading comprises a fierce responsibility, that the unfolding existence of the work depends on it:

Elle est ainsi littéralement une coopération, une collaboration intime, intérieure: singulière, suprême; une responsabilité ainsi engagée aussi, une haute, une suprême et singulière, une déconcertante responsabilité. C'est une destinée merveilleuse, et presque effrayante, que tant de grandes oeuvres, tant d'oeuvres de grands hommes et de si grands hommes puissent recevoir encore un accomplissment, un achèvement, un couronnement de nous . . . de notre lecture. Quelle effrayante responsabilité, pour nous.

It is this responsibility which validates the hyperbole of Heidegger's statement (a statement explicitly endorsed by Carne-Ross) that

Wir könnten mit Uebertreibung, aber mit ebensoviel Gewicht an Wahrheit, behaupten: das Geshick des Abend-Landes hängt an der Uebersetzung des Wortes 'εόν vorausgesetzt, dass die Ueber*setzung* in der *Ueber*setzung zur Wahrheit dessen beruht was in 'εόν zur Sprache gekommen.

(We can affirm with exaggeration, but with an equal weight of truth, that the destiny of the West presupposes the translation of the Greek word *being*. We can affirm that to translate translation into truth depends on how much of this Greek sense of *being* reaches language.)

Reflecting on the situation which I have just outlined and on the polemic between the stoic admonitors or mourners whom I have just cited and those who might be called the 'radical pastoralists', one or two very tentative conclusions might be worth putting forward.

The 'text' flourishes in a context of authority. Such authority can be of diverse sources. There is the metaphysical authority of a dogma or transcendent value-system. There is the pedagogic authority of an educational framework and consciously shared heuristic idiom. There can be political authority of every colour. These rubrics are, of course, interrelated. We have seen that 'textuality' and something of the quality and centrality of *lecture* as Péguy formulates it, do exist in the authoritarian fabric of the Marxist and Soviet community. There is here no paradox; Marxism being, in respect of its ideals of literacy and schooling, profoundly 'reactionary'. This is the crucial point. The insights of Péguy, like those of Heidegger, of Rieff and of Carne-Ross stem from a sharply conservative matrix. They derive directly from a tradition of élitist austerity and melancholy which dates, in its modern vein, from such ripostes to the Enlightenment and to the French Revolution as those of de Maistre and Julien Benda. Rieff follows immediately on Benda when he sees in the betrayal of the 'texts' in our academic-journalistic ambience the pre-eminent 'treason of the clerics'. There is in Carne-Ross's scruples, in the disenchanted exigencies of his model of education more than a hint of Newman's 'grammar of assent'. Heidegger's involvement with the totalitarian fantasies of German politics, both 'mystical-primal' and National Socialist, is notorious (though, in fact, too problematic and at some points, self-contradictory, to be dealt with summarily).

Even to face the issue of the correlations between genuine literacy and an authoritarian value-structure, is to repudiate out of hand the cant, the narcotic illusions, the cheery vulgarity of populist accent which characterize the current climate of cultural-educational argument in the West. We have to start by recognizing that there is no guaranteed congruence between the continued agency of classic or 'difficult' texts — such as have constituted our articulate culture and shared code of designation — and the pursuit of egalitarian or economically and socially redistributive ideals. It is not only that there is no guarantee of such congruence: the fact is that there is no eminent likelihood. The relations of the 'cultural' and of the 'democratic', of the 'classic' and of the 'socially just' are, at best, uneasy. They have, now and again, co-existed within a field of compromise and of consoling rhetoric underwritten by economic elbow-room, by the fact that there was no absolute need of a choice of priorities. Now times are harder and the inherent contradictions are made stark. 'Texts' are indeed inexhaustible to our needs, to that constant questioning and disinterested 'irresponsibility' of fundamental provocation which engenders original thought. But 'texts' are also initially and, sometimes, over a long period, 'closed'. Access to them is a matter of innate capacity and privileged environment, of· costly training and socially-insured leisure. How is the 'closed' text to prosper in the 'open' university? What concordance is realistically to be hoped for between the minority disinterests of the true reader and the demands for egalitarian satisfaction?

In short: any model of true reading (*une lecture bien lue*) is, fundamentally, a political model. And the politics of the 'text' are not, except in moments of great good luck and centrifugal largesse, libertarian.

Certain pragmatic conclusions do seem to follow. The attempt to impose 'textual' habits or a transcendental convention of the 'classical' on a mass public, as it is now being made in many of our universities, is a self-defeating hypocrisy. It must lead (it already has) to a rather tawdry opportunism or self-betrayal on the part of the teacher, and to indifference or extremism — which is the violent mask of boredom — on the part of the student. It is not only, as Rieff puts it, that 'behind the hippies come the thugs', a sequence to which the recent history of German universities has borne grim witness. It is that they come through doors flung open for them by gurus, trend-masters, arcadian didacts dizzy with the promise of a lasting shared youth. It is the professors in their forties, perhaps in search of personal erotic renascence, who have howled with the wolves and loudest.

Sadly, one cannot have it both ways. The fundamental correlations between 'text' and 'social context' are non-, perhaps anti-democratic. This has been the case in the high cultures of the past, and it is the case in Soviet existence today. Péguy argues from a ground of Catholic reaction; Rieff's and Carne-Ross's programmes or critiques are rooted in the ideals of hellenism and latinity as practised by an élite; Heidegger's intimations of the politics of deep literacy are blacker yet. I have tried to show in my own work that the 'humanities', in the sense in which the term inheres in 'classic humanism', do not entail any ready equivalence, any unforced co-existence with 'humanism' in a mass-liberal or socialist scheme of values. Creative literacy was always the disciplined, authoritatively transmitted possession of the few.

The general gloss which it gave to society, between the Enlightenment and the crises of the mid-twentieth century, sprang from power-relations, from pretences, from silences by the majority which our present world is no longer prepared to put up with.

One must, therefore, take the risk of positive contrivancies (it is the signal weakness of Rieff's polemic that he disdains to do so). If we want to preserve 'readers' in the old sense, *des lecteurs qui sachent lire* — this very wish being one that political and fiscal counteractions may render illusory — we shall have to train them, explicitly, laboriously, in a setting inevitably beseiged and, consequently, somewhat artificial. The problem is not one of ivory towers, but of the strength and cost of the material (elephants too are dying). We shall have to become at once exceedingly modest and exceedingly arrogant in our *profession*, in the syllabus of our *calling*, and restore to these terms something of their theological validation. The job to be done is not one of 'critical theory', of the 'sociology of literature', of, *mirabile dictu*, 'creative writing'. If we are serious about our business, *we shall have to teach reading.* We shall have to teach it from the humblest level of rectitude, the parsing of a sentence, the grammatical diagnosis of a proposition, the scanning of a line of verse, through its many layers of performative means and referential assumption, all the way to that ideal of complete collaboration between writer and reader as set out by Péguy. We shall have to learn to proceed, step by step, from the near-dyslexia of current student reading-habits to that enigmatic act of penetrative elicitation, the sense of the passage being perceived and in fact 'realized between the lines' as Heidegger instances it in his readings of Hölderlin. We will, simply, have to create universities or schools for reading.

He who teaches in such an institution has a job for life, but without tenure. His vocation must at all times be open to disproof, to the challenge (we must listen to it scrupulously though without fear) of those who regard the thing as not worth doing or, more cogently, as being intolerably costly in terms of social-political resources and goals. The real students in such 'houses of reading' — a phrase with Biblical precedent and promise — will be few, fewer perhaps than even the more sombre of our stoic seers would admit. The ironies, isolations, even falsities of the 'literate condition' will deepen. But if it is allowed to be done at all, the teaching, the transmission of tensed delight before the word, must be done proudly, *con amore*, or in that equally force-ful if eroded idiom, 'by heart'. If it is not done, if it lapses by cheapness or default, the 'text' will cease to be what, for some of us, it must be: the vital circumstance, the informing 'context' of our being.

2

On Difficulty

1978

What do we mean when we say: 'this poem, or this passage in this poem is *difficult*?' How can the language-act most charged with the intent of communication, of reaching out to touch the listener or reader in his inmost, be opaque, resistant to immediacy and comprehension, if this is what we mean by 'difficulty'? There is one obvious, crucial level at which this is a question about language itself. What is signified by the pragmatic experience that a lexically constituted and grammatically organized semantic system can generate impenetrability and undecidabilities of sense? No coherent answer could be given outside a complete model, such as we do not have, of the relations between 'thought' and speech, and outside a total epistemology, which again we do not have, of the congruence or non-congruence of speech-forms with a 'precedent' body of intention, perception, and vocative impulse. In such a model 'difficulty' would, presumably, be an interference-effect between underlying clarity and obstructed formulation. This, roughly, is the classical and Cartesian reading of opaqueness, a reading whose inference is necessarily negative. But all the relevant terms — 'inside'/ 'outside', 'intentionality'/'verbalization', and the crucial 'between' with its innocent postulate of a kind of mental space — are notoriously elusive. They activate a metaphor of separation and transfer about which neither logic nor psychology are in any agreement.

Our initial question is narrower; or, more precisely, it presumes a common sense intimation of continuities between linguistic intention and utterance. The individual reader or a group of readers find that they cannot understand this or that passage in a poem, or indeed the poem as a whole. How can such a situation arise? Even a cursory reflection suggests that when we say 'this text is difficult' we mean, or intend to mean, a number of very different things. The rubric 'difficulty' covers a considerable diversity of material and methods. These vary significantly in regard to literary genre and history. Thus it may be of some preliminary use to attempt a classification, a typology, of some of the principal modes of difficulty as one meets them in poetry, notably in Western poetry since the Renaissance. From such classification could derive a 'theory of difficulty' which remains one of the *desiderata*, made urgent by twentieth-century practice, in the·more general aesthetics of executive forms.

Very often, probably in the great majority of instances, what we mean when we say that a line of verse or stanza or entire poem is 'difficult' does not relate to conceptual difficulty. This is to say that our observation does not carry the same weight, that it does not have the same bearing, it would if we said 'this argument in Immanuel Kant, or this theorem in algebra is difficult.' (Though it is not altogether clear, epistemologically at least, just what it is that we mean in *these* cases. If algebra is the rigorous unfolding of previously-axiomatized definitions, if it is a dynamic tautology, what do we mean by saying that one or another step is 'difficult'?) But plainly enough, there is a difference. We may be aiming at something far less inherent or 'substantive' — a slippery term where languge is concerned — than concept.

Far more often than not we signify by 'a difficulty' something that 'we need to look up'. In what must be, statistically, the overwhelming plurality of cases, it will be a single word or a phrase which are not at once intelligible to us. Our resort to the authority of the dictionary is precisely analogous to that which we perform when translating from a foreign tongue. The word may be archaic: when Venus laughs on every *wight* in *The Merchant's Tale* or we meet with mighty *dints* in *The Knight's Tale*, we may no longer know what Chaucer is telling us. The obstacle may be one of dialect: that Warwickshire *mobled* which elicits Polonius's approval, or the Northumbrian *dingle* in which Auden finds darkness. The expression can be arcane and technical: it might not be immediately apparent to the reader just what 'bliss' T.S.Eliot promises when he qualifies it as *pneumatic* (the finesse lies in the Attic and theological antecedents to the epithet). Frequently, the poet is a neologist, a recombinant wordsmith: just what suave instrument had Mandelstam in mind when he invoked the music of the *tormenvox*? Writers are passionate resuscitators of buried or spectral words: to *disedge* fades after the early seventeenth century, but proves to be exactly what Tennyson requires to blunt 'The sharpness of that pain'. From Theocritus to the Edwardians, the manifold of exact denominations of fauna and flora is the cipher of western lyric poetry. It is now largely lost to our everyday awareness. Was Matthew Arnold quite certain whether he meant the plant of the genus *Fritillaria* or the species of butterfly, the silver-washed fritillary or the Queen of Spain, when he hailed the 'white and purple fritillaries by Ensham and down by Sandford?' Many of us, at least, will turn to the Oxford English Dictionary or the Royal Horticultural Society's invaluable *Dictionary of Gardening*. At certain moments in the history of poetry, *le mot rare* becomes the object of explicit pursuit and delight: to this day, Mallarmé's famous *ptyx*, one of the indispensable, sovereign rhymes in the sonnet on *ix*, appears neither in the Littré nor in the *Nouveau Larousse* (but it *can* be unmasked, via Greek and via liturgical art and this, as we shall see, is a key point). The below-ground vocabularies and syntax of slang, of argot, of taboo-usage, are sometimes almost as extensive and polysemic as those of mundane discourse. If a *monaker* was a guinea to the Victorian underworld, it was a proud ten-oared boat in the Eton College songs and odes of the day. To Thackeray an ass was a *moke*. Villon's idiom is, to a large measure, the rhyming cant and hieroglyph of thieves.

Poetry is knit of words compacted with every conceivable mode of operative force. These words are, in Coleridge's simile, 'hooked atoms', so construed as to mesh and cross-mesh with the greatest possible cluster of other words in the reticulations of the total body of language. The poet attempts to anchor the particular word in the dynamic mould of its own history, enriching the core of its present definition with the echo and alloy of previous use. He is an etymologist, often violent and arbitrary as was Hölderlin, who attempts to break open the eroded or frozen shell of speech in order to compel to daylight and release the dynamics, the primal crystallizations of perception that may lie at the roots. The poet's discourse can be compared to the track of a charged particle through a cloud-chamber. An energized field of association and connotation, of overtones and undertones, of rebus and homophone, surround its motion, and break from it in the context of collision (words speak not only to the ear, but to the eye and even to the touch). Multiplicity of meaning, 'enclosedness', are the rule rather than the exception. We are *meant* to hear both *solid* and *sullied*, both *toil* and *coil* in the famous Shakespearean cruces. Lexical resistance is the armature of meaning, guarding the poem from the necessary commonalties of prose.

The poem, in turn, is custodian of 'the holiness of minute particulars' (Blake's phrase). However abstruse the argument or universal the inference, the poet gives local habitation and name. Immediately past the obstacle of word or phrase, it is these we must look up. Mythologies, the names of stars, topography, the unnumbered furnishings of reality through which the poem incarnates and makes concrete. Because it is ontologically economical — another difference from prose — the language of the poem implicates a surrounding and highly active context, a corpus, possibly an entire world of supporting, echoing, validating, or qualifying material whose compass underwrites its own concision. The implication is effected by virtue of allusion, of reference to. The many-branched antennae which literally bristle outward from a line of Milton or Keats or Rilke to classical mythology are the precise contrary to dispersion. They make possible the compact largesse of the text; they embody the fully declared but unsaid codes and presences from which the poem draws its local generality. This is notably the case in Western poetry, so much of whose charged substance is previous poetry: Chaucer lives in Spenser who lives in Dryden who lives in Keats. The continuity inside these poetic visions, unbroken to the time of T.S.Eliot and of Robert Lowell, is that of specific 'elementals' and guarantors of felt meaning, namely Virgil, Horace, and Ovid, without whom the entire climate of recognitions on which our sense of poetic meaning is grounded would be hollow. But if other poetry is often the primary agent of context, so is, potentially at least, 'everything that is the case'. A poet can crowd his idiom, his landscape of motion, with the minutiae of history, of locale, of technical process (a key passage in *Hamlet* turns on the arcane technicalities of dyeing). He can cram hell, purgatory, and paradise with gossip so private that elucidation hinges on an almost street-by-street intimacy with thirteenth-century Florence. The occult node of vision may be just that: an eso-teric, a system of hermetic nomination and rites as in the poetry of Yeats. These several orders of difficulty, of that which needs to be looked up, constitute almost the entire fabric of Pound's *Cantos*, a meta-epic or parodistic epic whose essential tropes are those of inventory, private journal and almanac. At the close of Canto XXXVIII:

> Opposite the Palace of the Schneiders
> Arose the monument of Herr Henri
> Chantier de la Gironde, Bank of the Paris Union,
> The franco-japanese bank
> Francois de Wendel, Robert Protot
> To friends and enemies of tomorrow
> 'the most powerful union is doubtless
> that of the Comité des Forges,'
> 'And God take your living' said Hawkwood
> 15 million: Journal des Débats
> 30 million paid to Le Temps
> Eleven for the Echo de Paris. . . .

And granted that one's homework is done — that the ephemeral scandals of high finance in the steel and armaments industry, that the collusions between rotten republic and fascist empire, between bourse, bank and press, have been unravelled: what then of 'Hawkwood', not one suspects a fortuitous shard of private allusion, but a pointing to, a 'tuning towards' the characteristic dialectic of 'debate', of 'time' and of 'echo' in the lines following? To be looked up. As are the Greek tag and the high name of battle in one of the rapt sequences in Canto XXI:

> And after that hour, dry darkness
> Floating flame in the air, gonads in organdy,
> Dry flamelet, a petal borne in the wind.
> Gignetei kalon.
> Impenetrable as the ignorance of old women.
> In the dawn, as the fleet coming in after Actium
> Shore to the eastward and altered. . . .

And the looking up lies at the heart of the music; the one falls mute without the other. This is the point. Witness what is perhaps the epiphany, the leap to annunciation in the whole ramshackle majesty of Pound's design: the climax to the famous adjurations in Canto LXXXI:

> But to have done instead of not doing this is not vanity
> To have, with decency, knocked
> That a Blunt should open
> To have gathered from the air a live tradition
>   or from a fine old eye the unconquered flame
> This is not vanity.

Fair enough: but why 'a Blunt', and who is he? That proud old crank, Wilfred Scawen Blunt, and if so, what was there in his life and work to account for this luminous insertion?

This entire genus of difficulty and its main species conjoin in a fairly typical passage in the later style of Shakespeare — *Timon of Athens*, IV,3:

> O blessed breeding Sun, draw from the earth
> Rotten humidity: below thy Sisters Orbe
> Infect the ayre. Twin'd Brothers of one wombe,
> Whose procreation, residence, and birth,
> Scarse is dividant; touch them with severall fortunes,
> The greater scornes the lesser. Not Nature
> (To whom all sores lay siege) can beare great Fortune
> But by contempt of Nature
> Raise me this Begger, and deny't that Lord,
> The Senator shall bear contempt Hereditary,
> The Begger Native Honor.
> It is the Pasture Lards the rothers sides,
> The want that makes him lean: who dares? who dares
> In puritie of Manhood stand upright
> And say, this mans a Flatterer. If one be,
> So are they all; for every grize of Fortune
> Is smooth'd by that below. The Learned pate
> Duckes to the Golden Foole. All's oblique. . . .

'Grasp' in such a case is a concentric process, rippling outward from an immediate, almost instinctive, blurred apprehension ('I do know what this is about, in a sort of general way; the dramatic situation and certain key markers and emblematic sign-posts tell me') to successive levels of decoding. Of these, the first is purely lexical: depending on the degree of relevant literacy or familiarity with seventeenth-century diction, we find ourselves looking up, say, *orbe, dividant, rothers* (or should it be, as many editors emend, *wethers* or, as I suspect, an 'undecidable' active between both possibilities as they congrue in 'brothers?'), *grize, pate*. But 'purely' lexical is, of course, wrong. The truly arduous terms, those which Empson would cite in his studies of 'complex words', are *Nature, Fortune, Native Honor, Manhood* and, possibly, *Golden Foole* (leaving aside the intriguing question as to whether it is by Shakespeare's design that the First Folio alternates between upper and lower case with respect to 'Fortune' and 'Nature'). In rigorous turn, the probing of these words would lead from the dictionary and Shakespeare-concordance to the study of the very most dense, central topics in Elizabethan thought. It would lead to a study of the doctrine and metaphor of *fortuna* with its intricate background in antiquity and the Latin Middle Ages; to an investigation of the tight-meshed skein of abstract and imaged meanings around the concept of *natura*; to an analysis of the crucial but problematic notion of 'honor', an ambiguous notion in the light of Christian values, and one made even more many-valued here by Shakespeare's addition of *Native*. *Manhood* pivots on the whole renaissance paradigm of *virtu*, and one suspects that *the Golden Foole* has behind him those precedents of parable, of allegory, of archetypal figuration which provide the economy of Shakespeare's late manner with its resonance. And surrounding all these incarnate topics is the literal sphere of the Aristotelian-Boethian firmament with its 'Sister Orbes', its pharmacology of noxious exhalations, and its vehemently direct influence on the cosmic mysteries of 'procreation, residence, and birth' — a sphere, whose decipherment requires a fine understanding of medieval and

Renaissance systems of astronomy and astrology, together with some notion of the medical theory of 'humours'. Indeed, the invocation of the *breeding Sun* may point to more hermetic considerations, to those filaments of Gnostic and alchemical belief which so often brush the far edges of Elizabethan and Shakespearean cosmology.

Homework: mountainous, and becoming more so as our twentieth-century brands of literacy recede from the vocabulary, from the grammars, from the grid of classical and biblical reference which have mapped the contours of Western poetry from Caxton and Chaucer to the archival gathering or museum-catalogue in *The Waste Land* and the *Cantos*. Homework which is, in a real sense, interminable, as there is always more 'to look up' (what reticulations are dynamic in the possibility that *grize*, the single step or stair in a flight, chimes with 'graze' as on a 'Pasture', and is a variant on *grece* with its evident pointers to 'Lards' and to 'smooth'd' in the line following?). 'Looking things up' does not stop because the context pertinent to a major poem or poetic text is that of the whole ambient culture, of the whole history of and in the language, of the mental sets and idiosyncracies in contemporary sensibility. (The issue is philosophically vital: a language-act is inexhaustible to interpretation precisely because its context is the world.) Moreover, there is an inevitable feed-back: with every particular clarification, comes a motion of return to the poem. What we have looked up of Elizabethan teachings on astral influence works back on our reading of Timon's monologue. It makes that monologue richer, which is to say that it raises new questions: what, for example, was Shakespeare's own addendum to or variation on the prevalent picture of the origins and kinship, literal and allegoric, of sun and moon?

In practice, the homework of elucidation may be unending. No individual talent or life-span, no collective industry, can complete the task. But *not in theory, not formally.* This is my point. Theoretically, there is somewhere a lexicon, a concordance, a manual of stars, a *florilegium*, a pandect of medicine, which will resolve the difficulty. In the 'infinite library' (Borges's 'Library that is the Universe') the necessary reference can be found. Walter Benjamin suggests that there are cruces and talismanic deeps in poetry which cannot be elucidated now or at *all* times; they were understood formerly, they may be rightly glossed 'tomorrow'. No matter: in some time, at some place, the difficulty can be resolved. Conceivably, the distance between a culture and certain texts can grow so drastic that *everything has to be looked up* (this is almost the case when a twentieth-century student tries to read Pindar, say, or Dante or certain stretches of Milton). In practice this may make the given text inaccessible; it slips over the horizon of pragmatic perception as do the retreating galaxies. But the point *is* pragmatic, not ideal or theoretical. Granted time and explicative means, even *everything* can be looked up. I suggest, therefore, that we label this first class of difficulties (statistically by far the most compendious class) as 'epiphenomenal' or, more plainly, as *contingent* difficulties. In the overwhelming majority of cases, what we mean by saying 'this is difficult' signifies 'this is a word, a phrase or a reference which I will have to look up.' In the total library, in the *collectanea* and *summa summarum* of all things, I can do just that. And find that a *ptyx* is a conch.

Contingent difficulties are the most visible, they stick like burrs to the fabric of the text. Yet we may find ourselves saying 'this is a difficult poem' or 'I find it difficult to grasp, to place this poem' (the shift into a first-person register of experience is, here, significant) even where the lexical-grammatical components are pellucid. We have looked up

what there is to look up, we have confidently parsed the elements of phrase — and still there is opaqueness. In some way,
the centre, the rationale of the poem's being, holds against
us. The sensation is almost tactile. There is, at empirical
levels, 'understanding' — of the rough and ready order represented by paraphrase — but no genuine 'comprehension',
no in-gathering in the range of senses inseparable from the
archaic Greek *legein* (to 'assemble', to 'enfold in meaningful
shape'). The experience of obstruction is at once banal and
elusive. A move in American slang, though already somewhat
dated, may pinpoint the cardinal distinction: we 'get the text'
but we don't 'dig it' (and the suggestion of active penetration is
exactly apposite). The poem in front of us articulates a
stance towards human conditions which we find essentially
inaccessible or alien. The tone, the manifest subject of the
poem are such that we fail to see a justification for poetic
form, that the root-occasion of the poem's composition
eludes or repels our internalized sense of what poetry should
or should not be about, of what are the intelligible, morally
and aesthetically acceptable moments and motives for
poetry. The poem enacts language in modes we find illicit;
there is radical impropriety between its performative means
and what we take to be the spirit, the native pulse, the constraints of the relevant tongue or idiom. Here the notoriously
abbreviated and therefore elusive Aristotelian notion of 'propriety', of that which is proper to a given poetic genre, would
be pertinent.

Again, to be sure, there is one sense, at least, in which this
type of difficulty is referential. The poet may have left an
explanatory statement telling us what he is about, what his
intentions and formal co-ordinates were. There may be a
document which will clarify the occasion or anti-occasion of
the poem's composition. But even then, we may find that the
region of difficulty has only been displaced or better defined.

The process of 'looking it up' does not lead to an un-ambiguous solution; or, more precisely, it falls to one side of the operative distinction between surface-understanding or paraphrase on the one hand, and penetrative compre-hension on the other. The objection would now be this: 'are you not confusing what you call genuine insight with merely aesthetic judgment? Are you not muddling questions of difficulty with those of taste?' The overlap is undoubtedly there, and the nuances are blurred. Nevertheless, there is a real discrimination to be made: as between our pleasure in or displeasure at something that we have thoroughly apprehended, and our reaction to, our atrophy of response towards a text whose autonomous force of life, whose *raison d'être* in the strict sense of the phrase, escape us. We have done our homework, the sinews of the poem are manifest to us; but we do not feel 'called upon', or 'answer-able to', in both of which tags the primary bonds of inter-action between the poem and its listener or reader are active. And it is just because this failure of summoning and response can lie wholly outside the categories of 'liking' or 'disliking' that it is not, or not only, a question of taste. The diffi-culty which we are up against is of a class which I propose to call *modal* (a term used by C.S.Lewis). I can instance it with regards to Lovelace's fifteen-line lyric, *La Bella Bona Roba*:

> I cannot tell who loves the Skeleton
> Of a poor Marmoset, nought but boan, boan
> Give me a nakedness with her cloath's on.
>
> Such whose white-sattin upper coat of skin,
> Cuts upon Velvet rich Incarnadin,
> Ha's yet a Body (and of Flesh within).
>
> Sure it is meant good Husbandry in men,
> Who do incorporate with Aëry leane,
> T' repair their sides, and get their Ribb agen.

> Hard hap unto that Huntsman that Decrees
> Fat joys for all his swet, when as he sees,
> After his 'Say, nought but his Keepers Fees.
>
> Then Love I beg, when next thou tak'st thy Bow,
> Thy angry shafts, and dost Heart-chasing go,
> Passe *Rascall Deare*, strike me the largest doe.

Contingent difficulties swarm; but they are tractable. Once we know that a *bella bona roba* is Caroline argot, very likely of Venetian provenance, for a 'whore', much falls into place. *Marmoset* is tricky, but the various senses and intonations center on somthing like a small monkey or emblematic grotesque known for lechery. The whole lyric pivots on the dual meaning of 'venery' as sexual chase and the hunt of animals — a twinning as old as the myth of Meleager and heavily routine in European love-poetry and erotic satire from the twelfth century on. Hence the twofold agency of *Huntsman*, of *Say* (for 'assay'), of the *Keepers Fees* (referring simultaneously to the brothel and to the huntsman's tract of woodland or moor), of *Bow* (hunter Cupid), of the *angry shafts*, which are both 'arrows' and, to this day, 'phallus', and the obvious play on *Heartchasing* and on *Rascall Deare* — a technical term signifying a particularly lean animal. Another routine turn is that on *Husbandry* in the sense of economy and conjugality. This line of duality is taken up in the allusion to Adam's rib, whose excision has left men bereft. Quite evidently, the text energizes and elaborates on a richly-available stock of verbal-emotive congruencies between eros and the slaying of game. Thus *a nakedness*, the *white-sattin upper coat of skin*, the velvety carmine beneath it, and the motif of gauntness in *boan, boan,* in *Aëry leane*, the contrastive *Fat joys* and the *Rascall Deare*, meld the woman's bone and flesh with that of the slain quarry. But these elements, all of which are subject to 'being looked up' and verified by analogy with a host of Petrarchan and contemporary verse, do not take us very far. There is something palpably un-settling, even repellent, about the movement and lunge of the whole poem. The order of difficulty is not removed by clarification of word and phrase. It functions centrally.

Another circuit of reference seems to be in Lovelace's text, at a covert, 'in-group' level — a set of intimations that lies behind the tried and public carapace of sexual con-noisseurship. If I am 'hearing' rightly, and one is obviously on very tentative ground, there is some sort of witty, marginally blasphemous dialectic being sparked off around the two poles of Adamic and New Testament incarnation. The mystery of the flesh and of its waxing and waning is vividly present: in *Skeleton*, in *boan, boan*, in *nakednesse*, in *Incarnadin* (which, of course, contains the radical for 'flesh'), in the open proposition on *a Body (and of Flesh) within*. But also, and with what may be a glance at the paradox of transubstantia-tion, in *incorporate*. 'Carnality' with its liturgical over- and under-tones, is insistent. If Adam and Eve are present in the structure so, one begins to suspect, is Christ, whose carnal self-revelation and self-sacrifice is so explicitly a counter to Adam's fall, and the spear-thrust in whose ribs is so manifestly a counter-*figura* to Adam's loss from which all evils sprang. It is these awesome changes that would appear to be rung on that haunting phrase: *Who do incorporate with Aëry leane.* In short: what we have before us is a brilliantly-turned, burnished Cavalier lyric, whose ostensible matter is one of sexual prescription: 'do not lose your *swet* and *Keepers Fees* on a bony whore; pick a girl in the Rubens vein.' The generalizing title may well refer to a particular woman or erotic contretemps in Lovelace's circle. Already, we may be sensing difficulties of a *modal* sort: is this piece of gamy advice, this roué's tip, the kind of occasion and locus for poetry with which we can engage at any but the cerebral level? Is this the class of experience and concern which poetry is readily about? Is the substratum of sensibility, the nonchalant identification of woman's flesh with the deer's carcass, one that is still in reach of our feelings? But even as we pose these questions, their inadequacy shows itself to be crass. So much more is going on in the text. The rhetorical acrobatics are so evidently out of tune with an underlying current of concentrated, possibly clandestine association. Is it theological? One is not certain. And if it is, at what remove do we post ourselves and our reading from a style of language and a climate of consciousness in which venery and transubstantiation mesh? Here, there are no answers to be 'looked up'. Which is, precisely, what distinguishes a contingent from a modal difficulty.

Current man seeks to efface this distinction. Heir to Rousseau, our culture professes to know less but to feel more than any before it. We may have to look up even the most elementary of scriptural, mythological, historical, literary or scientific terms and references; but we claim confident empathy with Benin bronzes, the shadow-dramas of Indonesia, the ragas of India and every genre and epoch in Western art. Ours is now Malraux's *musée imaginaire* in which collage and reproduction make possible the juxtaposed intimacy of the archaic and the romanesque, the primitive and the surreal. We are ashamed to concede any modal inhibition, to confess ourselves closed to any expressive act however remote from our own time and place. But this ecumenism of receptivity is spurious. It deliberately confounds the reconstructive acquaintance achieved by virtue of knowledge and archaeology of feeling with authentic apprehension, with penetrative inscape. Learning, the suspension of reflex, can make us understand *at the cerebral level* the dynamics of judgment which made of Rosa Bonheur a painter far more highly valued than Cézanne or which induced Balzac to set the novels of Mrs. Radcliffe above those of Stendhal (whom he was one of the first to praise). But we cannot coerce our own sensibility into the relevant frame of perception. Large, sometime radiant, bodies of literature have receded from our present-day grasp. Who now reads, who experiences at any adequate depth of response, the tragedies of Voltaire, which once dominated the European canon of tragic drama from Madrid to St. Petersburg, or the high dramas of Alfieri that came after? A substantial measure of European literature from the sixteenth to the later nineteenth centuries drew constantly and with intimate recognition on the epic poetry of Boiardo, Ariosto, and Tasso. It was in this poetry that writers as diverse as Goethe, Keats, and Byron found a primary body of reference and instigation. European art and music are ubiquitous with the presence of Rinaldo and Angelica, of the distracted Orlando and Armida's garden. To mid-twentieth-century literacy this entire syllabus of sentiment and allusion is either a closed book or the terrain of academic research. Now it is only the scholar who knows that Ariosto is one of the two or three acutest witnesses of the nature of war in the whole of moral history, that he stands with Homer and Tolstoy among the few who have assessed the ambiguous profits of combat in the economy of human affairs. But his idiom and orders of apprehension are no longer natural to us. The difficulty is modal and it is real.

Contingent difficulties arise from the obvious plurality and individuation which characterize world and word. Modal difficulties lie with the beholder. A third class of difficulty has its source in the writer's will or in the failure of adequacy between his intention and his performative means. I propose to designate this class as *tactical*. The poet may choose to be obscure in order to achieve certain specific stylistic effects. He may find himself compelled towards obliquity and cloture by political circumstances: there is a very long history of Aesopian language, of 'encoding' and allegoric indirection in poetry written under pressure of totalitarian censorship (oppression, says Borges, is the mother of metaphor). The constraints may be of a purely personal nature. The lover will conceal the identity of the beloved or the true condition of his passion. The epigram, be it Martial's or Mandelstam's, will be couched in terms translucent to the few, but initially closed to the public eye. But there is also, and often decisively, an entire poetic of tactical difficulty. It is the poet's aim to charge with supreme intensity and genuineness of feeling a body of language, to 'make new' his text in the most durable sense of illuminative, penetrative insight. But the language at his disposal is, by definition, general, common in use. Its similes are stock, its metaphors worn down to cliché. How can this soiled organon serve the most individual and innovative of needs? There have, throughout literary history, been logical terrorists who have taken the implicit paradox to its stark conclusion. The authentic poet *cannot* make do with the infinitely shop-worn inventory of speech, with the necessarily devalued or counterfeit currency of the every-day. He must literally create new words and syntactic modes: this was the argument and practice of the first Dada, of Surrealists, of the Russian 'Futuro-Cubist' Khlebnikov and his 'star-speech'. If the reader would follow the poet into the *terra incognita* of revelation, he must learn the language. In effect, to be sure, this logic of the occult is autistic. A secret tongue will not communicate outward, and if it loses its mystery, if it is acquired by many it will no longer contain the purities of the unprecedented. The position of the radical but working poet is, therefore, a compromise. He will not forge a new tongue but will attempt to revitalize, to cleanse 'the words of the tribe' (Mallarmé's famous formula gives pointed summation to what is, in fact a constant compulsion in poetry and poetics).

He will reanimate lexical and grammatical resources that have fallen out of use. He will melt and inflect words into neological shapes. He will labour to undermine, through distortion, through hyperbolic augment, through elision and displacement, the banal and constricting determinations of ordinary, public syntax. The effects which he aims at can vary widely: they extend from the subtlest of momentary shocks, that unsettling of expectation which comes with a conceit in Metaphysical verse, to the bewildering obscurity of Mallarmé and the modernists. The underlying manoeuvre is one of *rallentando*. We are not meant to understand easily and quickly. Immediate purchase is denied us. The text yields its force and singularity of being only gradually. In certain fascinating cases, our understanding, however strenuously won, is to remain provisional. There is to be an undecidability at the heart, at what Coleridge called the inner *penetralium* of the poem (there is a concrete sense in which the great allegories of ingress, of pilgrimage to the centre, such as the *Roman de la rose* and the *Commedia*, compel the reader to re-enact, in the stages of his reading, the adventure of gradual unfolding told by the poet). There is a dialectical strangeness in the will of the poet to be understood only step by step and up to a point. The retention of innermost meaning is, inevitably, subverted, and ironized by the mere fact that the poet has chosen to make his text public. Yet the impulse is an honest and crucial one, arising from the intermediate status of all language between the individual and the general. The contradiction is insoluble. It finds creative expression in tactical difficulties.

When Michelangelo addresses Cavalieri, he pounds the rubble of Petrarchan phrases and conceits into fantastic shapes:

> Si amico al freddo sasso é 'l foco interno
> che, di quel tratto, se lo circumscrive,
> che l'arda e spezzi, in qualche modo vive,

> legando con sé gli altri in loco etterno.
> E se 'n fornace dura, istate e verno
> vince, e 'n più pregio che prima s'ascrive,
> come purgata infra l'altre alte e dive
> alma nel ciel tornasse da l'inferno.

The initial crux is that of ardent flame somehow vital inside cold stone, then blazing out of the stone and circling it with fire (*se lo circumscrive*); thus making of the rock or marble what is literally a living ash or mortar (*in qualche modo vive*) by virtue of which other stones can be knit (*legando con se gli altri*) into a form that will endure everlasting (*in loco etterno*). If it can resist the furnace's heat, stone will the more readily vanquish summer and winter (*istate e verno vince*). Doing so, it will acquire a worth beyond its own first nature (*più pregio che prima*), as does the soul that has returned purified, burnt clean (*purgata*) from a sojourn in hell and heaven (*alte e dive*). The trope unfolds in the closing triplet in which the poet, now made smoke and ash (*fatto fummo e polve*), sees himself as ever-enduring (*etterno ben saro*), precisely because of his reduced impalpable state, but then, in a closing line which remains unclear, images himself as hammered not by iron but by gold (*da tale oro e non ferro son percosso*). The counterpoint of matter and spirit, of flame and ash, together with the implicit 'plot' which recounts the lover's fiery reduction by the desired brilliance of the beloved, are the stale props of the Petrarchan idiom. Michelangelo injects into them the tactile vehemence of his own incomparable intimacy with stone and hammer, and the kindred presence of Dante whose *Commedia* is a persistent referential touchstone in Michelangelo's *Rime*. The tactical difficulties spring from, are intended to make manifest, the fact that Michelangelo's feelings for Cavalieri are of such intensity and genuineness that they can make use of the most banal counters of expression. Like others in the garland, this sonnet enacts its own central motif: it consumes and scatters to rubble (*l'arda e spezzi*) the material of which it is constituted — the Petrarchan diction — in order to give to that material the mystery of fresh and lasting life.

Already, Góngora seems to prefigure Mallarmé, by his subversion of the common linearity of syntax, by his nominalization of adjectival and adverbial forms. In the sonnet which he addresses to the Flemish painter of his portrait (the painter is unknown, the picture has disappeared), Góngora is poised midway, as it were, between the neo-Platonic and Petrarchan *topos* of identity and image, a *topos* routine to Michelangelo, and Mallarmé's paradoxalities on the 'presentness' to the spirit, to the 'sensoriness of the spirit', of that which is absent:

> Hurtas mi bulto, y cuanto más le debe
> a tu pincel, dos veces peregrino,
> de espiritu vivaz el breve lino
> en las colores que sediento bebe,
> vanas cenizas temo al lino breve,
> que émulo del barro le imagino,
> a quien (ya etéreo fuese, ya divino)
> vida le fió muda esplendor leve.

In the Michelangelo text, everything is harshly palpable, even the flame has edge. Here all is diaphanous and mobile. Again, the secret scandal is that of art which can confer on the most ephemeral of substances (*el brevo lino*) by means of *esplendor leve*, a nearly unrecapturable phrase in which the sumptuousness and the extreme lightness of the painter's touch is rendered, the *espiritu vivaz* of being. This intangible being takes on the needs of carnal life: the canvas drinks the colours (*las colores que sediento bebe*) as men drink water or — surely the allusion is active if deep-buried — as the shades of the departed drink ritual libations of life-blood in order to become present to us. But though intense, the 'substantive image' on the canvas stays mute: *vida le fió muda*. Which condition makes of a painter's portraiture of a poet a peculiarly peremptory seizure (*hurto*). *Dos veces pere-grino* is tantalizing: why is the painter's brush 'twice pere-grine'? What is its twofold pilgrimage? Is Góngora invoking the Platonic paradigm of the twofold remove of art from the archetypal Forms, its double descent, via *mimesis*, into counterfeit? We are meant to hesitate, to have only gradual, earned access to the crowning paradox of the sonnet, that that which sees, which hears, lasts less (*quien más ve, quien más oye, menor dura*), a paradox in which the living poet salutes the scandalous survival of his own mute image and conjoins the Platonic with the Scriptural meditation on the ephemeral nature of sensory existence. But observe the paradox within the paradox: the salute to the enduringness of the impalpable is spoken to a painting, itself a wholly perishable, material genre. The painting itself will only last if it can steal the 'bodily spirit' of the sitter. And thus the spiral of equivocation begins again.

It may be no accident that tactical difficulties crop up where poets consider their métier. 'Contingently' and 'modally' Wallace Stevens's 'Anecdote of the Jar' is trans-parent:

> I placed a jar in Tennessee,
> And round it was upon a hill.
> It made the slovenly wilderness
> Surround that hill.
>
> The wilderness rose up to it.
> And sprawled around, no longer wild.
> The jar was round upon the ground
> And tall and of a port in air.
>
> It took dominion everywhere.
> The jar was gray and bare.

It did not give of bird or bush,
Like nothing else in Tennessee.

The aesthetic proposition is unambiguous: however simple ('gray and bare'), the work of art reorganizes, sets ordinance upon the surrounding chaos of the organic. The ministration is as antique and imperative as was Orpheus' song: like the forest and beasts crouching to hear the singer, the wilderness gathers around the jar 'no longer wild'. The mildly ceremonious, archaic 'port in air' confirms the classic note. In turn, the motif of a central circle and of a verticality within it, plays on subliminal, possibly archetypal recognitions of order, on intimations patent in art and dreams of how the inchoate world is given sense. It is the last two lines that obstruct and unsettle. The immediate obtrusion is that of syntax: 'give of' and 'like nothing else' are either a regional idiom or ungrammatical. There is deflection within deflection as 'to give of' seems to call naturally for 'like anything else'. Yet the 'nothing' is so obviously purposed. So far as I am aware, no reading of the text has come up with a coherent parsing or equivalent transposition into normal syntax. To transpose, to paraphrase into correctness, is to relinquish both the motion and the meaning of the poem's meaning. At one level, and not trivially, we do know, we do 'make out' what Wallace Stevens is saying. The artifact transmutes the organic into the organized, but is not of it. It works via detached centrality. It is itself sterile — 'it does not give' as does the vegetable or the animal presence of 'bird or bush'. It has no affinity with them — if one reads 'to give of' as analogous to such normal forms as 'to smell of', 'to sound like'. In this solipsistic integrity, the jar is unlike anything else in Tennessee. All else in 'the slovenly wilderness' is meshed and partakes of a shared providence ('to provide' signifying to 'give of itself'). The jar dominates uniquely but is, by definition, empty ('bare' enforces this implication of lofty vacancy). 'Anything else' would vulgarize the crux of singularity. The 'nothing', with its arrest of rhythm, enacts the requisite twofold motion of extreme differentiation — 'nothing is like the jar' — and of inherent 'nothingness'. But Wallace Stevens's allegory is a radical critique of the proposition abundant in *King Lear* that 'nothing shall come of nothing'. The charged 'nullity' of art centres and cultivates reality.

We can arrive at this reading by a sort of semantic approximation. We cannot demonstrate or paraphrase it grammatically. As we move with and against the anti-grammar of the two lines, the effect on us is that of moiré, of the meaningful but unstable and reticulating patterns in shot silk. There is a distinct sense in which we know and do not know, at the same time. This rich undecidability is exactly what the poet aims at. It can be made a hollow trick (as it often is with the syntactic instabilities in Dylan Thomas). Or it can serve as a true tactical difficulty, forcing us to reach out towards more delicate orderings of perception. It is, simultaneously, a subversion and energizing of rhetoric drawing attention, as poets such as Michelangelo, Góngora, and Wallace Stevens do persistently, to the inertias in the common routine of discourse.

Contingent difficulties aim to be looked up; modal difficulties challenge the inevitable parochialism of honest empathy; tactical difficulties endeavour to deepen our apprehension by dislocating and goading to new life the supine energies of word and grammar. Each of these three classes of difficulty is a part of the contract of ultimate or preponderant intelligibility between poet and reader, between text and meaning. There is a fourth order of difficulty which occurs where this contract is itself wholly or in part broken.

Because this type of difficulty implicates the functions of language and of the poem as a communicative performance, because it puts in question the existential suppositions that lie behind poetry as we have known it, I propose to call it *ontological*. Difficulties of this category cannot be looked up; they cannot be resolved by genuine readjustment or artifice of sensibility; they are not an intentional technique of retardation and creative uncertainty (though these may be their immediate effect). *Ontological* difficulties confront us with blank questions about the nature of human speech, about the status of significance, about the necessity and purpose of the construct which we have, with more or less rough and ready consensus, come to perceive as a poem.

Ontological difficulties, certainly in the modern vein, seem to have their history: they are the object of theoretical argument and stylistic manipulation in the hermetic movement that relates certain elements in Rimbaud, the poetics of Mallarmé, the esoteric programme of Stefan George, Russian formalism and futurism, and the dependent impulses which have come after. To ask why *ontological* difficulties should come to be seen as a *desideratum* or inescapable fatality in European literatures of the late nineteenth and early twentieth centuries, is to ask an absolutely fundamental question about the crises of idiom and values in the entirety of modern Western culture. A summary reply would be fatuous. The aetiologies of this inspired movement towards darkness are as various as the individual talents and social circumstances involved. Certain broad contours do stand out. The transformation of the visionary elements in the Enlightenment and French Revolution into the philistine positivism of the industrial and mercantile structure of the nineteenth century, brought on a drastic mutual disenchantment of artist and society. Severed from concrete revolutionary possibilities, later romanticism cultivated the posture of inward exile, of the poet's isolation in a prosaic society. This stance entailed an essentially private ideal of communication. At the same time, the rapid proliferation of journalistic and popular media of communication — the press, the *feuilleton*, the cheap book — while beneficial to prose fiction, accentuated the minority status of the poem. With this industrialization of language and of the means of dissemination of language came the semi-literacies characteristic of a technocratic and mass-consumer society. To certain poets — and it is at this node that Poe occupies a position much in excess of his intrinsic merits — the ancient trope of inadequate discourse, the conceit whereby words fall short of the unique immediacies of individual experience, became a more general issue. Now it was language as a whole that was being cheapened, brutalized, emptied of numinous and exact force, by mass usage. This view is implicit in Baudelaire, in Gautier's quest for the rare, unsullied word, in Verlaine's ideal of musicalization. It becomes programmatic in Mallarmé's resolve to cleanse the vocabulary and syntax of common speech, to carve out and preserve for poetry an arcane realm of uncompromising significance.

But behind these motives, complex and multiple as they are, two even deeper instincts or conjectures seem at work. The first is that of an almost subconscious insurgence against the mountainous authority of the classical past, against the hectoring traditionalism which informed high literacy since the Renaissance. In the hermeticism of poetry after Mallarmé there is an attempt, not untinged with irony, to shake off the constraints of influence and of public-academic expectation based on the canonic (much in Mallarmé is a revolt, only partly successful, against Victor Hugo, and against the fanfares of eloquence in which Victor Hugo proclaimed his own kinship with the eternal accomplishments of the prophets, of Dante, of Shakespeare). To become esoteric was to break the chain of exemplary inheritance. The second impulse is, on the contrary, one of reversion, of an attempted return to an archaic past in which languge and thought had, somehow, been open to the truth of being, to the hidden sources of all meaning. This motion is explicit in Mallarmé's dictum of 1894 that all poetry has 'gone wrong' since the magisterial, but ultimately erroneous, achievement of Homer. By becoming linear, narrative, realistic, publicly-focused, the art of Homer and his successors — this is to say of the near totality of Western literature — had lost or betrayed the primal mystery of magic. Mallarmé's examplar of this magic is Orpheus who, like the jar in Tennessee, casts the net of order over the organic world, and who descends to the heart of death via the spiralling staircase of his song. These are the crucial trials of poetry, and they lie outside Homer's 'realistic' and informational purpose. In the late 1920s, Heidegger gave historical-philosophic vogue to a precisely parallel reading of the Western condition. In the riddling fragments of Parmenides, of Heraclitus, of Anaximander, thought and saying are a perfect unity. The *logos* stands 'in the clearing of being', gathering to itself the 'hidden presentness of Being in beings', the quiddity of autonomous existence and meaning towards which Gerard Manley Hopkins had bent his vision. What Homer is to poetry in Mallarmé's model, Plato and Aristotle are to the Heideggerian diagnosis of the 'amnesia of true Being' in Western rationalism. If it is the task of the true poet to force his way upstream to the Orphic sources of his art — and where there is compulsion there will be difficulty — it is the task of the thinker, of man in his essence, to return to the illuminations of authentic existence reflected in the pre-Socratics. In Heidegger's view, it is the poet-thinker Hölderlin who has, until now, come nearest to communicating to us the nature of this homeward turn. Radical modernism in European poetry is, I believe, largely derived from Mallarmé's practice and from Heidegger's theoretic metaphor, and from the image of Hölderlin in Heidegger. In *ontological* difficulty, the poetics of Mallarmé and Heidegger, of the Orphic and the pre-Socratic, express their sense of the inauthentic situation of man in an environment of eroded speech.

These attitudes coalesce in the mature poetry of Paul Celan — to which fact must be added the specific discomforts of a survivor of the holocaust writing poetry comparable in stature to Hölderlin's and Rilke's, and poetry of the utmost personal compulsion, in the butchers' tongue. 'Largo', from the volume *Schneepart*, is by no means uncharacteristic:

> Gleichsinnige du, heidegängerische Nähe;
> über—
> sterbens—
> gross liegen
> wir beieinander, die Zeit—
> lose wimmelt
> dir unter den atmenden Lidern,
>
> das Amselpaar hängt
> neben uns, unter
> unsern gemeinsam droben mit—
> ziehenden weissen
>
> Meta—
> stasen.

There are, to be sure, difficulties here of the kind we have looked at before (and it is at these that any attempt at translation, such as Michael Hamburger's, will take a stab). *Heidegängerisch* seems to play, as Celan's later verse frequently will, on the name of the philosopher and on the Heideggerian concept of the *Feldweg*, the peregrination through, the traverse of, open country; *Amsel*, signifying 'blackbird' (as does the name of Kafka who is a perennial titulary presence) closely echoes the actual name of the poet, for which 'Celan' was an anagram; the title 'Largo' invites the conjecture that the *Meta-stasen*, the 'attendantly passing white clouds' may imply some mode of musical rest and (?) the great librettist Metastasio. There is a profound but intelligible twist in *über-sterbens-gross* which plays on the normal *überlebensgross*: side by side, the lovers are 'larger-than-death', literally 'transcendent' in the 'almost-repose' and immobility, at once erotic and suggestive of sepulchral effigy, in 'metastasis'. P.H.Neumann's *Wort-konkordanz zur Lyrik Paul Celans bis 1967* shows that *die Zeit-lose* and the use of *Lidern* to crystallize the presence of the beloved, are recurrent and talismanic in the poet's work. But no concordance can give access to the private net which Celan spins around *Zeit*, in which strands of annihilation and survival are equally and simultaneously meshed, or to the map of meaning implicit in the identification between clouds and *Meta-stasen*. There is, therefore, and centrally, an action of semantic privacy. It is not, as in the case of *tactical* difficulties, that we are meant to understand slowly or to stand poised between alternatives of signification. At certain levels, we are not meant to understand *at all*, and our interpretation, indeed our reading itself, is an intrusion (Celan himself often expressed a sense of violation in respect of the exegetic industry which began to gather around his poems). But again we ask: for whom, then, is the poet writing, let alone publishing?

This paradox is inseparable from ontological difficulty, and was already the object of incensed argument around Mallarmé. For whom was the Master composing his cryptograms? If one leaves to one side the strategies of historical circumstance — Mallarmé's campaign for a purification, for an 'aristocratization' of poetic idiom, Paul Celan's anguish at writing poetry, at having to write poetry 'after Auschwitz' and in the language of the devisers of Auschwitz — ontological difficulty seems to point to a hypostasis of language such as we find, precisely, in the philosophy of Heidegger. It is not so much the poet who speaks, but language itself: *die Sprache spricht*. The authentic, immensely rare, poem is one in which 'the Being of language' finds unimpeded lodging, in which the poet is not a *persona*, a subjectivity 'ruling over language', but an 'openness to', a supreme listener to, the genius of speech. The result of such openness is not so much a text, but an 'act', an eventuation of Being and literal 'coming into Being'. At a naive level, this image yields the suspect expressionistic tag that 'a poem should not mean but be'. At the more sophisticated but equally existential level, it generates the poetics of 'dissemination', of 'de-constructive' and 'momentary' reading that we find in Derrida and the current school of semiotics. We do not 'read' the poem in the traditional framework of the author's *auctoritas* and of an agreed sense, however gradually and gropingly arrived at. We bear witness to its precarious possibility of existence in an 'open' space of collisions, of momentary fusions betwen word and referent. The operative metaphor may be that crucial to Mallarmé's famous *L'absente de tous bouquets*, to the modern physicist's determination of 'the unperceived event' in the cloud-chamber, and to Heidegger's equivocation on the 'absence in presence' (the play on *Ab-* and *Anwesen*). In each case the observable phenomenon — the text — is the inevitable betrayal, in both senses of the term, of an invisible logic. Yet we do know that the Mallarmé *envoi* or the Celan lyric *is* poetry, and often major poetry. We do know that we are not looking at nonsense or at planned obfuscation, as in the case of certain Dada and surrealist collages. 'Largo' is a profoundly moving statement, though we cannot say confidently or paraphrastically 'of what'. How do we have this assurance, what allows us to discriminate, even within the class of ontological difficulties, between the necessary and the factitious, and even between 'the real' and the 'more real' (a differentiation which might bear on the distinctions to be made between, say, Rilke's difficulties in the *Duino Elegies* and Celan's)? This seems to me one of the most urgent questions in the whole of aesthetics and of the modern attempts at a philosophy of meaning.

The subject of difficulty in poetry, in art, is as large as are the performative means of language and of visual and aural expression. It has moved to the very centre of aesthetic experience since the late nineteenth century. Neither aesthetic theory nor general public feeling have coped with it satisfactorily. It is, as yet, impossible to say whether the hermeticism of so much in the modernistic movements is a transient phenomenon or represents some ultimate break in the classic contract between word and world. The classification into contingent, modal, tactical and ontological difficulties put forward here is, obviously, rough, and preliminary. But it would be unusual if any of the difficulties actually met with in poetry, and in literary texts as a whole, were irreducible to one of these four types or to the manifold combinations between them.

3

A Remark on Language and Psychoanalysis
1976

The raw material *and* instrumentality of Freudian analysis are semantic — a duality which poses serious epistemological dilemmas. In one respect, at least, Freud's lifelong hope of neurophysiological 'evidence' and confirmation, a hope unrealized, can be construed as a desire for escape from the hermeneutic circle of language seeking to deal systematically with language. But there was no escape. The original and classic psychoanalytic process cannot operate if the patient is mute or the analyst is deaf (a restriction both more comprehensive and more singular than might at first appear).

The semantic material used by Freud in his theoretic writings and *praxis* derived from written and from oral sources — an obvious configuration which, however, becomes a 'three-body problem' (notoriously insoluble) due to the fact that Freud is himself a major writer with relations to the German language of a sort and complexity which distinguish the great stylist. The influence of this personal register on Freud's 'hearing' and 'reading' is a topic as yet unexplored. I will not be touching on it here, but it is present in my remarks by active implication.

The written material on which Freud principally draws is that of the Central European syllabus of high literacy as taught and categorized in the period *c.* 1870–1920. It includes and articulates an axiom of continuity from the Greek and Latin classics to the modern masters. It assigns a pivotal, numinous centrality to Homer, Sophocles, Virgil, Shakespeare, Cervantes, a centrality compacted, as it were, in the genius, at once conservative and creatively syncretic, of Goethe (it is the Orphic fragments *Über die Natur*, wrongly attributed to Goethe, which convert Freud to his vocation). The nineteenth-century novel, notably from Balzac to George Eliot, Flaubert and the Russian masters, is seen as a continuation of the commitments to human realities and individual character present already in the classic tradition. To this syllabus, Freud's Central European contemporaries will add, and give canonic status to, the achievement of Ibsen.

It is not only that Freud derives his illustrative material from this canon with an innocence or immediacy so trusting that it leads to the analysis of dreams dreamt inside the poem, drama or novel: it is that Freud treats his literary texts as having *evidential* force. Let me adduce only three cases among many: the recourse to Jocasta's 'many a man hath lain with his own mother' and to Diderot's *Neveu de Rameau* to substantiate the Oedipus complex; the identification of coitus with sensations of ascent as demonstrated in Daudet's novel *Sappho*; and the polarization of 'corrupt beauty' and 'virtuous ugliness' in two female characters in George Eliot's *Adam Bede*.

But it is the overall point which needs emphasis. In Freud's work, texts from Sophocles, Shakespeare, Rousseau, Goethe, Ibsen, E.T.A.Hoffmann, Balzac, Dostoevsky, Jens Peter Jakobsen, Schnitzler and Strindberg (to name only the major sources) are given evidential 'clinical' status. This attribution embodies a very particular 'classical' view of the *auctoritas* of literature. Yet Freud also has complex, ambiguous responses to just this view.[1] There is a genuine contradiction here: literature is privileged 'truth' but also a transitional phenomenology on the way to 'maturity' and to a full acceptance of the reality-principle. Secondly, this attribution of *auctoritas* embodies a particular view of language (literature being language maximally charged).

[1] Cf. that intricate, uncertain paper on 'Creative Writers and Day-dreaming' published by Freud in 1908.

This view of language overlaps with, is reinforced by, the oral semantic material which Freud assembles in his personal and social life and in the actual process of analysis. Here again the important point to be made concerns the specificity, the linguistic-social historicity and even localization of the material. Freud is a Viennese Jew, in an intricate phase of arrested assimilation with its own very special semantic strategies. His circle is that of other Viennese Jews or of the emancipated Jews and half-Jews coming to Vienna from the very particular language-spaces of Budapest-German and Prague-German. (The Freud-Jung letters are a formidably rich document in respect of the resulting semantic tensions, as between Jewish-Viennese-German, with its aspiration to the 'purities' of Lessing and Goethe, and the German of a gentile whose own Zürich variety of the vulgate was vulnerable.)

Moreover, to a degree on which we urgently need further statistical verification, the speech-acts which Freud listens to and analyses are those of the more or less leisured middle class, of a Viennese-Jewish middle class, and of women. Each of these parameters — the social, the ethnic, the sexual — is language-specific in profound and manifold ways. As Reich pointed out, the middle-class habits of discourse on which Freud drew are themselves only a small, contingent element of the total spectrum of verbalization. The Jewish speech-world is, in some regards, extremely idiosyncratic. The 'grammar' of women is not that of men.

The consequences of this historical specificity have never, I believe, been fully grasped, nor, I think, has psychoanalysis quite faced the paradox inherent in the foundation of a universal, normative model of meaning and behaviour on so local a semantic base.

Sigmund Freud's understanding and use of language enacts and incorporates the following *données*:

(a) The patient is highly articulate. His utterance-inhibitions are blockages, pathologies of latent abundance. He uses language in an economically prodigal, possibly inflationary way (as distinct from laconic tactics and cultures).

(b) The patient's articulacy is polysemic and vertically-structured. He knows several words for the same object; he knows that the same word has several meanings. He is cognizant, even if only at a subliminal level, of the play of connotation, denotation, ambiguity, which surrounds the word and even the individual morpheme with a dynamic multiplicity. Of this multiplicity jokes, puns, play on words, slips of the tongue — all of which are indispensable to the Freudian analytic process — are manifest expressions. But although such polysemic attributes and dislocations are a part of every natural language, the operative areas of taboo, social dialect, historical and local reference in which they occur, are cultural-specific. Freud's reading of the covert meanings and witticisms in the analytic material, his emphasis on portmanteau-words and elisions, are inseparable from the speech-habits and particular idiolects of Central European middle-class Judaism in its final historical phase.

(c) Of these speech-habits, that of reference is crucial. Freud's patients are not only fluent and polysemic, they are literate in the true sense. They have read and they have remembered. The result is a specific density of interior echo, of allusion, of misquotation (the most famous of which is Freud's own 'I vary Hamlet's remark about ripeness — cheerfulness is all' in the seminal letter to Fliess of 21 September 1897,[1] when Freud means to cite the word 'readiness' and is, in fact, thinking not of *Hamlet* but of *King Lear*). The dreams which Freud analyses are of literature and of the literate. The underlying life of language is, for Freud, shot

[1] S.Freud, *The Origin of Psycho-Analysis. Letters to Wilhelm Fliess, Drafts and Notes: 1887–1902* (London, 1954).

through with cultural associations of that special classical —
Central European legacy to which I pointed earlier. Analysis
draws neither on the inarticulate nor on the unlettered (there
is in Freud's refusal to deal with psychosis a terror before the
inchoate, before the semantically-closed, as deep as was the
terror in Goethe's choice of 'injustice rather than disorder').

In short: it is not free association which generates the
Freudian language-evidence, but association organized, even
at its deeper levels, by the context of utterance and reading
of a very particular milieu at a very particular moment in
European cultural history. The resultant model of language
and of meaning, with its entailment of verticality and of decipherment 'from above' is, inevitably, a part of this history.
Thus Freud's hermeneutic — and what is psychoanalysis if
not a branch of the 'science of understanding'? — stems
naturally and fully from two sources: from Talmudic exegesis,
the Judaic assumption of the spirit hidden and instrumental
in the letter, and from the German hermeneutic tradition of
Schleiermacher, Dilthey and their successors in the *Geistes-
wissenschaften* (which very term, untranslatable into English,
articulates that notion of an 'exact science of the spirit',
exact but not in quite the same way as the neurophysiological
sciences, which both attracted and worried Freud during his
entire career).

Small wonder that no contemporary analyst meets any
patients who sound like those of Freud. Men and women no
longer speak as did the Central Europeans, the Central
European Jews, the Central European Jewish women of the
turn of the century. They no longer read the classics, let
alone quote or know them by heart. The literacy of our
dreams has altered radically.

Jacques Lacan's famous paper of 1953,[1] deemed by some

---

[1] J.M.Lacan, 'Fonction et champ de la parole et du langage en psychanalyse',
Psychanalyse 1 (1956), 81–166.

to be the one major theoretic advance since Freud himself, can be interpreted as an attempt to transcend the vulnerable 'localism' of Freud's linguistic commitment.

Lacan postulates that psychoanalysis will either establish its foundations in an adequate linguistics or have no serious foundations at all. Its concept and empirical usage must orient themselves *'dans un champ de langage'*, and must do so in ways consonant with the semantic investigations of modern philosophy (e.g. Frege), of modern linguistics (e.g. Saussure and Chomsky) and of modern anthropology (here it is Lévi-Strauss whom Lacan has principally in view). *La parole du patient* is the sole medium of psychoanalytic action whether the latter be heuristic, epistemological or therapeutic. But to call this *parole* 'free association' is, says Lacan, a 'humorous ruse'. It is the task of the analyst, as it is that of the logician, linguist and anthropologist, to discover the deep-lying structures and constraints of the patient's *discours*, for only in this perspective can the psychoanalytic claims to scientific generality and to an evolutionary dynamic be validated. Hence Lacan's central notion of a *discours concret transindividuel* of which the unconscious is a lacuna, a gap which the patient must fill in order to re-establish the continuity of conscious speech. Hence also his assertion, the influence of which has already been great, that the pathological condition which psychoanalysis addresses itself to, 'resolves itself wholly in a language-analysis, because the symptom is itself linguistically structured, because it is itself a language the enunciation of which (*parole*) must be brought to light (*délivrée*).'

It follows that the unconscious is 'structured', that it has a syntax, precisely in the sense made familiar to us by the deep-structure postulates of transformational generative grammars and by the Lévi-Straussian model of binary symbolic arrangements underlying all social and aesthetic forms of human understanding and activity. The prohibitions of incest on which Freud bases his account of the germination of culture cannot antedate the linguistic *pouvoir de nomination* which, itself, embodies the structural, grammatically-relational fabric of the human psyche. This leads Lacan to a rigorously Saussurian formulation, that the archetypal psychoanalytic problem is that of the *rapport dans le sujet de la parole et du langage*. The elucidation, the therapeutic restoration of this *rapport* depends on an understanding of the symbolic edifice, of the symbol-generating processes which constitute the unconscious and which are translated into the syntax of speech.

Lacan's strategy is twofold. He would give to the classical Freudian scheme of hermeneutic verticality a more rigorous (i.e. abstract, logistically formal) and a more universal base. He recuperates, but on a far more astute, sophisticated basis, the Freudian desideratum of neurophysiological location, by inferring a psychic 'space' or spatialization with a high degree of organization. (Lévi-Strauss makes the same inference when he hints at the crucial role of the hemispheric division of the brain in all binary codes.) Simultaneously, Lacan seeks to regain the ground lost, damagingly I think, to anthropology — Freud never met the Malinowskian challenge which was made, precisely, on the ground of the parochialism of Freud's evidence — and to Jung. By extending the notion of language to include, to be rooted in, overall symbolic operations, Lacan allows the relevant presence of symbolic forms which are 'coded' but not necessarily linguistic in Freud's sense. Lacan's concept of 'the semantic or semiotic' is, therefore, at once more abstruse and flexible than that of Freud.

I have elsewhere[1] argued substantive disagreements with the doctrine of 'deep structures' on which the scheme of

[1] G.Steiner, *Extraterritorial* (London and New York, 1971); *After Babel* (London and New York, 1975).

Lacan, like that of Chomsky, is founded. I have tried to suggest that its inferences of exactitude are either unproven or of a formally trivial order, and that much of Lacan's idiom, itself so opaque, is concealed metaphor (e.g. when he uses *archives* for memories, when he plays rich changes on the fashionable notion of *écriture* or of 'punctuation' when he means the end of the analyst's hour etc.) Nevertheless, Lacan is, I believe, absolutely right when he states that psychoanalysis is an applied linguistics and when he seeks to provide this application with dimensions of reference far beyond those of the original Freudian material. The proposal, moreover that the unconscious is relationally structured, and that it is this architecture which determines or over-determines its connexions with conscious feeling and speech, seems to me to be, in the best sense, seminal. Provided, that is, that we recognize the significant part of metaphor in such concepts as 'structure' and 'relation'.

These marginalia should indicate some of the inextricable meshing of language and psychoanalysis. But another approach, from 'outside', may be worth considering.

Of necessity, 'information theory' and the great bulk of psycholinguistics and sociolinguistics bear on public, externally enunciated speech. The implicit paradigm is one of source-transmission-reception. As we know, however, 'spoken speech' constitutes only a part of the totality of discourse. It may well be, even on a statistical basis, that internal speech, the current of language which we address to ourselves or which constitutes the incessant pulse of thought and dreams, accounts for much the greater segment of the semantic whole. Despite the omnipresence of this interior speech-milieu, not very much is known about its evolutionary history or what may be the particularities of its grammatical, lexical form. If the early Piaget is right, internal speech precedes audible, public utterance, passing from a first stage of 'autism', through 'egocentrism' to a gradual apprehension of and response to the outside world. Vygotsky argued otherwise, suggesting that internal language is a relatively late borrowing from external discourse, and that its aetiology relates to the individual's discovery of a hostile or 'non-answering' reality.[1] The argument remains unsettled. But it may be worth asking whether there is not, from the evolutionary start, a considerable difference between external articulation, with its informational and societal functions, and the very different, often counterfactual and fictive character of internal discourse. The sociological dimension is also problematic. Eighteenth-century observers maintained that genuine internal speech is an attribute of literacy: the unlettered move their lips when speaking to themselves.

As introspection, the study of speech-disorders and psychoanalysis have shown, internal speech can go very deep indeed. It touches on every facet of personal experience. But there have been a number of domains in which 'silent language' has exercised a dominant function.

Much of religious sentiment and performance is verbally internalized in the guise of prayer, invocation, supplication, self-admonition or penitential scrutiny. It is only when an individual addresses himself to the deity that one can speak of a 'monologue with'. This paradoxical rhetorical mode postulates a presence whose very silence does not negate the communicative act, but somehow confirms it, making of the monologue a dialectric structure. In his *Mémoires* Saint-Simon notes that only an absolute monarch can soliloquize out loud, his essential apartness being such that those who may, by chance, overhear him have no real existence. The observation is subtle and suggestive. The ordinary man must conduct his monologue internally, and in the process of

[1] L.S. Vygotsky, *Thought and Language* (Cambridge, Mass., 1934, 1962).

prayer it is the most absolute of kings who is silently implicated.

Sexuality is yet another sphere in which interior speech plays a major part. Self-arousal and satisfaction generate powerful streams of unspoken verbal material. The actual erotic experience will often have been verbally programmed, prefigured beforehand. Coitus itself may be accompanied by a mute commentary, often subversive of the apparent tenor of external tone and behaviour. Obscenity has led a rich life below the taboo-line of socially-permitted enunciation.

But whatever its psychic depth, interior language is subject to the influence of historical change; or, to be more exact, the relations of proportion and intensity as between exterior and interior speech are subject to such change.[1]

What evidence we have suggests that the religious content of internal verbalization has sharply diminished, certainly in Western culture. Journals, texts of meditation, manuals and exercises of self-examination and penitence, the liturgical practices and aids as we know them from the fourteenth to the early eighteenth century, point to a wealth and discipline of unspoken discourse of which we, today, have only the vaguest notion. The believer of the seventeenth century (here the documents are of particular density) spent hours in articulate meditation on God and the self. The inward current of his discourse was precisely focused. It had the stringency of analytic argument and debate, not the patchwork logic of daydreaming. Buttressed by silences and a schooling of memory such as our own culture has largely lost, the interior monologue of the Cartesian or Pascalian speaker will have advanced its clarities and demands to the threshhold of the unconscious.

The transformations in the relative spheres of erotic speech have been equally radical. It is the current dispensation to

[1] These are discussed in the following essay.

'say all', to externalize and publish modes of idiom which, previously, and certainly so far as the 'genteel' classes went, had been reserved either for silent utterance or for moments of ultimate, shared privacy. What words, what turns of phrase, cannot be used today out loud, or on the stage, or in print? The two devaluations — that of religious and that of erotic language and internality — are obviously related. Together they amount to an almost programmatic 'thinning out' of the interior medium. Indeed, I would be tempted to define crucial aspects of modernity in terms of the drastic reduction of internal language and of the concomitant inflation of public verbalization, of 'publicity' in the full sense of the term.

Psychoanalysis has been the beneficiary and is now an agent of this dislocation. It arose at a moment in the history of European sensibility in which the techniques of focused introspection and self-interrogation had withered away. It provided a secular, though heavily mythological, surrogate for an entire range of introspective and elucidatory disciplines extending from private meditation to the meta-privacies of the confessional. Psychoanalysts gave institutional licence to the outward articulation of what had formerly been the preserve of internal speech. For complex motives, which involve the initial strength and subsequent breakdown of Puritan practices of self-purgation as well as the striving for the most rapid possible integration of different ethnic and social groups, American civilization has witnessed the greatest shift from inner to outer speech. It is, therefore, no accident that in America the fortunes of psychoanalysis should be the most spectacular. Psychoanalysis is a craft of directed externalization. Whatever Freud's own stoic commitment to a constraint-ideal of civilized existence, the positive valuation which psychoanalysis gives to articulate saying, to *Aussprache*, is overwhelming. Though it claims as its therapeutic aim the reconstitution of a proper economy of internal resources, psychoanalysis, by virtue of its process, erodes the autonomous energies of inward diction and plenitude. One does not need Kierkegaard to remind one that where a secret has been dislodged and published, a kind of malign emptiness remains.

The liberations which Freud initiated are, of course, immense. To grow up after Freud is to be enfranchised from a spectre-host of unnecessary terrors, hypocrisies and idolatries. Psychoanalysis has, without question, restored to self-acceptance and varying degrees of social efficacy many who would otherwise have receded into desperation (though, in fact, the concept of a psychoanalytic 'cure' remains uncertain). But the cost of this emancipation and of the general movement of externalization of which it is only a part, is rarely assessed.

The 'voidance' (the archaic word is difficult to replace) of inner spaces of coherent discourse has shifted fundamental ballast. We are off-balance under stress, less lodged in ourselves (characteristically, the American house is, or was until very recently, open to all comers). Speaking all, our media of communication seem to say less. Overhearing everything, our listening has grown less acute. What current psychology provides the exact fineness of internal reception, the scrupulous discriminations of perception across deepening planes of silence and near-autism, which made possible the descent into the self of St.John of the Cross, of Pascal, even of so modern a listener as Amiel? There are crazily-shaped, almost monstrous creatures who survive in the great deeps of the sea. Brought to the surface, they burst or shiver into inert powder. The same is often the case when analysis teases into open utterance and daylight the shaping pathologies, the vital cancers of internal language.

In a verse which is untranslatable, because the strength in it of interior statement is so intractable and, at the same time, audible, Hölderlin says that genuine speech, as distinct from noise or tautology, can only exist *wenn die Stille kehrt.* Paraphrase is fatuous, but he seems to be teaching us something absolutely central about the 'return', about the 'homecoming' of the human word to its internal roots, about the intricate equilibrium between utterance and the unsaid. Hölderlin's programme and that of psychoanalysis are, necessarily, at odds. The mental derangement — *Umnachtung* is a truer word — to which Hölderlin succumbed or which he took upon himself (our aetiological classifications being in such a case wholly naive) is relevant, no doubt. But in what way?

4

The Distribution of Discourse
1978

Lévi-Strauss and other anthropologists conjecture that there are loquacious, word-spendthrift cultures, and cultures which are avaricious of speech and hoard language. This hypothesis is nearly impossible to verify. But obvious as they are, the obstacles to verification point to significant concepts and composites of opaque material. How would one define, for purposes of quantification, the sum of speech, of linguistic communication, of enunciatory action by verbal means, in a given society and at a given moment? What is the word-count of articulate exchange or discourse during a twenty-four hour period for any 'speech-unit' or 'social-semantic clustre' of two or more human beings? Suppose we devised acoustic and tabulatory equipment capable of registering all speech-sounds in a determined time and place (such equipment has in fact been used to study some of the temporal variables in the flow of telephone messages). Would the numerical result be of any significance? There might be non-trivial points of comparison, as between social classes, the conspicuous consumption or retention of words as between men and women, the differing economics of verbal investment and output as between age-groups. Though it would pose delicate problems of interpretation (are the time and place chosen representative of the standard of speech-habitats, what corrective or constant ought one to introduce into the speech-curve in order to adjust to the differential weight of a highly-developed, polysemic or allusive idiom as compared with more rudimentary monosyllabic conventions of diction, and so on?), the evidence might be well worth having. Yet even with the most sophisticated controls, such a summation and distributive analysis of verbal events would be radically incomplete. The most sensitive electronic count would register and tabulate only *external* speech.

With the exception of L.S.Vygotsky (whose investigations bear essentially on the genesis of linguistic competence in the very young child), linguists have given almost no thought to the formal characteristics, statistical mass, psychological economy or social specificities of *internal* speech. How often, under what lexical, grammatical and semantic categories and constraints, at what rate of flow, in which language (where the polyglot is concerned) do we speak to ourselves? Are there meaningful discriminations to be made between those modes of soliloquy in which there is a greater or lesser degree of attendant labial motion and those in which there is no such motion, at least at the observable level? Merely to pose these questions is to realize that inward speech is the *terra incognita* of linguistic theory and of psycholinguistic and sociolinguistic positivism. It is precisely the absence of a competing linguistic theory or body of experimental data which has provided the psychoanalytic language-model of Freud and of Lacan with a crucial area of contrivance. A reflection on the nature and history of human speech, a theoretical-statistical account of semantic totality, could well begin with the premise that the major portion of all 'locutionary motions', this is to say of all intentionalities of verbalization, whether audible or not, is *internalized*. This premise would lead to a number of fruitful inquiries.

The initial area would be genetic and motivational (the two being inseparable). The large majority of mythological and scientific conjectures on the origins of language posit the unexamined axiom of inter-personal communication. Whether in Hesiod, Humboldt or J.Monod, we find the implicit or enunciated supposition that the evolution of human speech is concomitant with, generated by, or creative of trans-individual societal behaviour. Through speech men communicate with one another, and such communication is the indispensable requisite and motor of all social or higher forms of action. The mutation to speech, with its reciprocal interactions as between function and capacity in the cortex, establishes man's humanity and pre-eminence in the organic order. The development of language would thus have been, in the Darwinian sense, the supreme adaptive advantage. Verbal exchanges between human speakers construct an informational environment more powerful and dynamic than that of nature. Indeed we have seen recently the growth of the concept of 'informational thermodynamics' in which the informational 'bit', with its analogues all the way from the alphabet, phrasing and punctuations of the genetic code to the most complex forms of language, would constitute the prime unit of energy.[1] Again the underlying axiom or model is societal, the current of articulate energy is outer-directed.

This need not be the case. It is entirely possible to envisage an evolutionary scenario in which the dynamics of survival would entail the early development of inner-directed and intra-personal address. Myths of mutual nomination, such as that of Jacob and the Angel, or of ordeals of self-identification and designation, such as that of Oedipus (both types being, I believe, variants on the same motif) seem to point towards a problematic, possibly millenially prolonged development of and struggle towards a working notion of singular identity (in schizophrenia, in the numerous pathologies of *dédoublement*, this notion is again subverted or made recessive). The confident scission between self and other, between 'I' and 'you', may well be an arduous, late achievement whose underlying

[1] Cf. L.Brillouin, *Science and Information Theory* (London, 1962); *Scientific Uncertainty and Information* (London, 1964).

economics are dialectical. Autonomy is diacritical to reciprocity. So that there can be semantic exchange distinguishable from echo there must be a determination of integral source. It may be that such determination is underwritten by speaking to oneself before, during or after linguistic encounter with another. Such monologue need not be unvoiced. The self-oriented or apparently objectless chatter of the very young and the very old may be a recapitulation of primal patterns of address. A whole range of causalities or conditions is conceivable: we speak to ourselves in answer to a limitless variety of external or somatic stimuli (hope, fear, self-castigation, self-encouragement); we speak to ourselves in order *not* to speak to others (the ubiquitous fairy-tale motif of those who whisper their compelling secrets into mute wells or under rocks illustrates one of the relevant mechanisms); we speak to ourselves to anchor our own presentness, to ground the threatened or elusive sense of self (soliloquy in the dark, in shock); we speak to ourselves to store the acquisitions of experience, to hoard and make inventory (to what degree is the history of the evolution and incision of memory, in its early stages at least, a history of self-address, of literal deposit by articulate import? The *ars memoriae* of the Renaissance is a branch of rhetoric); we speak to ourselves when engaged in language-play, this is to say in any of the manifold and disinterested — non-utilitarian, non-focused — modes of phonetic, lexical, syntactic experiment and transformation which are characteristic of the child, of 'automatic speech' or of poetry (a poem is first said inward). Each of these orders of motive or occasion is complexly functional in respect of the origins and conservation of the ego. In evolutionary terms, internal speech, in some probationary guise possibly related to the slow development of the neurophysiological instrumentalities of articulation, may have preceded external vocalization. Or it may have evolved as a necessary correlative to it. Or it may have come *after* public utterance as an absolutely essential safeguard of identity and of the private spaces of being (we will return to this point). Whatever the evolutionary chronology and intricacies of interaction, internal speech-acts are as important as external, societal speech-acts, and it is very likely that they represent the denser, statistically more extensive portion of the total distribution of discourse.

Can one trace this polarization in the growth of the individual? The most stimulating discussion on this point remains that between Vygotsky[1] and Piaget, who replied to Vygotsky's critique in 1936. Vygotsky held that in their ontogenetic development thought and speech have different roots. In the linguistic growth of the child, he found a pre-intellectual stage; correspondingly, there is a pre-linguistic stage in thought development. Up to a certain point in time, the two follow different and independent lines. It is when these lines converge that thought becomes verbal and speech rational. Differently from Watson,[2] Vygotsky found no evidence that inner speech develops in some mechanical way through a gradual decrease in the audibility of external utterance (the child's resort to whispering in his third or fourth year). Instead he proposed a three-phase model: external speech, egocentric speech, inner speech. In the latter 'the external operation turns inward and undergoes a profound change in the process. The child begins to count in his head, to use "logical memory", that is, to operate with inherent relationships and inner signs. In speech development this is the final stage of inner, soundless speech'. This development necessarily depends on outside factors. It is the child's exploration of the social aspects and functions of language that leads to the development of logic on which inner speech is based. Hence Vygotsky's conclusion that 'verbal thought is

[1] L.S.Vygotsky, *Though and Language* (Cambridge, Mass., 1934, 1962).
[2] J.Watson, *Psychology from the Standpoint of a Behaviourist* (New York, 1919).

not an innate, natural form of behaviour but is determined by a historical-cultural process and has specific properties and laws that cannot be found in natural forms and thought and speech'. All our observations, argues Vgyotsky,

> indicate that inner speech is an autonomous speech function. We can confidently regard it as a distinct plane of verbal thought. It is evident that the transition from inner to external speech is not a simple translation from one language into another. It cannot be achieved by merely vocalizing silent speech. It is a complex, dynamic process involving the transformation of the predicative, idiomatic structure of inner speech into syntactically articulated speech intelligible to others.

Thus inner speech is not the interior aspect of external speech. In it, according to Vygotsky, words die as they bring forth thought. It is a 'thinking in pure meanings. It is a dynamic, shifting, unstable thing, fluttering between word and thought, the two more or less stable, more or less firmly delineated components of verbal thought'. Below and beyond it lies the plane of 'thought itself'. In his concluding remarks, Vygotsky calls for an as yet unformulated 'historical theory of inner speech'.

One need not accept the entirety of Vygotsky's paradigm, with its methodologically and evidentially vulnerable emphasis on preverbal, pre- and extralinguistic 'thought', to appreciate the value of his focus on inner speech and the importance of the notion of an 'historical theory of inner speech'. The present essay is intended as a provisional and rudimentary contribution towards such a theory. It elides the substantive and terminological issues raised by Vygotsky's binary scheme of 'thought' and 'language'. It takes 'inner speech', the unvoiced soliloquy, the silent monologue, to signify and include all internalized motions of statement, whether these derive from a simple suppression of outward vocalization ('I am saying to myself that which I wish not or dare not say out loud') or from subconscious, 'pre-verbal' sources. What it seeks to stress is the application to internal speech-phenomena of the concept of historicity.

   Merely to say this is to perceive that if we have histories of *la langue*, this is to say histories of the lexical and grammatical features which constitute the diachronic morphology of a human tongue, we have none of *la parole*. We know next to nothing of the genesis, institutionalization, transformations in the speech-conventions and habits of historical societies except in those highly specialized cases in which such conventions and habits are codified by writing (leaving aside, for the moment, the difficult question of the degree to which written forms ever codify the speech milieu in which they are composed). We do not know, or know only through the distorting glass of the written text, what men and women in a given historical time and place regarded as comprised in the areas of articulate verbal communication and what they regarded as 'inexpressible' for reasons which can range the whole way from mystical illumination to social taboo. What could one talk about or not talk about? If we seek to compare two communities or historical epochs, what can we surmise of their respective speech prodigalities or parsimonies? In the antique Mediterranean world, the Greeks were a byword for loquaciousness. It was said of the Romans (but the sources here may be suspect precisely because they are mostly Roman) that they cultivated laconic modes of utterance and prized taciturnity. What is the contrastive evidence worth, and would it allow even the crudest of quantifications (just how many more words 'flowed' in a Greek house or in the *agora* than in a Roman domestic setting or in the *forum*?). To stick with this one example for reasons of illustration: suppose the general report to have been valid, what of the crucial phenomena of repartition as between sexes, age-groups or social classes? Certain Greek women — precisely those few of whom literary and social anecdote has record — were celebrated for their eloquence. The Roman code, on the contrary, is that crystallized in Shakespeare's rendition of Coriolanus' greeting of Virgilia: 'My sweet silence, hail'. Recent scholarship, however, suggests that there were key spheres of activity — economic, familial, even religious — in which Roman women exercised a more forceful, more articulate role than did their Attic counterparts, and Juvenal's Sixth Satire does not seem to point to feminine quietness in the imperial city (we possess no history of noise-levels, of the decibels of word-volume in which different generations, societies and communities within the same societies have conducted their daily lives). What of children? Rule-of-thumb testimony, memoirs, the tales of travellers, adduce a mass of evidence on the subject. We are told of societies in which the child is incited to speak early and copiously, in which the babble of children is a source of adult satisfaction and amusement. Other periods and societies (the Lutheran manse, the Victorian brownstone) are characterized as repressive in respect of children's speech and voices. Here the rewards of adult approval go to extreme sparseness of response or silence. Chateaubriand's memoirs tell of an atavistic feudal milieu in which young children and even adolescents were bound to strict silence between late afternoon and the ritual, monosyllabic reply to parental benediction and dismissal at bedtime. How much temporal and geographical ground does such an account comprise? What of the servants' quarters? Quite obviously the statistics of speech-production and distribution have social determinants. It is in the nature of the case that almost all written records of linguistic behaviour stem from the literate and the privileged. 'History' has made mute the preponderant part of mankind. But in at least one cardinal domain, that of sexual speech, what evidence we have strongly suggests that the less literate and underprivileged classes of society, both urban and rural, knew a license and wealth of accepted expression entirely inadmissible in middle- and upper-class contexts. Erotic taboos in language are class-bound. A laconic surface or ideal of linguistic consumption can have beneath it a spendthrift argot. Reciprocally, periods and societies whose literary achievements imply a formidable resource of lexical, grammatical and semantic means, may in fact be founded on underpinnings of inarticulacy and even silence. What were the contrasts of articulacy as between the Elizabethan élite and the *beau monde* of the French eighteenth century on the one hand, and the respective mass of the rural population on the other? What was the average vocabulary and syntactic range available to the Castilian peasant at the time of Cervantes and Góngora?

What, moreover, are the causalities of change, the agencies of transformation which affect the 'locutionary total' of a given culture? The complexity of factors and uncertainty of evidence are such that it is difficult even to phrase one's questions plausibly. Even as it is among the most constant and ubiquitous of human acts, so speech is among the most susceptible to the modifications of the biological and social environment (it is probably an error to keep these two apart). There are intricate, deep-felt contiguities between obscurity and silence on the one hand and loquacity and light on the other. One of the principal metamorphoses in human affairs has been that brought on by the altering equation between the hours spent in darkness and those spent in light. To an extent often unnoticed by social historians, the great mass of mankind passed a major portion of its life in the varying shades of opacity between sundown and morning. The history of artificial lighting, from the palaeolithic hearth-fire to the neon of the modern metropolis, with its virtual muta-tion of night into a 'counter-day', cannot be separated from that of consciousness itself. In what ways have the conventions and statistics of linguistic exchange been modified by the voluntary prolongation of the lit portions of existence? Correlatively, in what respects has the evolution of the habitat, from open and collective spaces to the closed and even individual room — an evolution itself subject to crucial climatic, economic, sexual and ideological variants — affected the occasions, critical mass, volume and styles of discourse?

All these and a host of analogous questions pertain to what the French historians now call *l'histoire des mentalités* and of which Febvre's investigation of the sense of smell in sixteenth-century sensibility or Vovelle's attempt to map changing attitudes towards the remembrance and commemoration of death in a given community and religious-economic milieu, are pioneering examples. Because it is itself the dominant instrument of any such inquiry, the linguistic text and what can be gathered from oral traditions is often taken as an axiomatic constant. In fact, the modalities of language vary as complexly in dimension, form and distribution as do the data of human experience and conception which they embody. And if this is true of external speech, it is equally true of inner and inward speech. In short, the phenomenology, of self-address is itself historical. If the audible speech acts of cultures, social classes, genders, age groups and epochs change under the pressures of inheritance and environment (inheritance *is* environment) so do the inaudible, the internalized, the autistic. Even more than that 'historical theory of inner speech' asked for by Vygotsky, we need some idea of what the material for and towards such a theory would be.

This essay aims to initiate lines of thought on what appears to be a radical shift in the relative density and tenor of external and internalized speech-forms in the literate segments of Western society between the seventeenth century and the present. It derives from the critical postulate that certain genres of writing are peculiarly related to inward discourse and give warrant of its prolixity. It might be profitable, on another occasion, to review this postulate in some detail.

The generation and emission of language by the individual both enacts and mirrors the power relations, the conventional and contingent hierarchies in the social unit. In middle- and upper-class families of the classic age, lines of force were manifestly concordant with primacies of age, gender and public station. Initiation of verbal activity, whether inquisitive, prescriptive or generally propositional seems to have been one of the unexamined prerogatives of men as distinct from women, of parents as distinct from children, of masters as distinct from servants (it is just the inversion of this latter code which creates the comic, challenging element in Molière's depictions of articulate, vocally peremptory servants and halting masters). The currency of words was largely minted and issued by the senior masculine presence in the given familial unit. The recurrent idealization, in poetry, in manuals of good conduct, in homiletic texts, of the softness of voice of 'good women', is a certain indicator of the privileged loudness of men. Conversely, we can document the suspicion largely held and enunciated in plays, satires and moral tracts that women, when among themselves, when out of masculine earshot, would literally erupt into conspicuous prodigalities of speech. The scenario is one of intense polarization by virtue of gender and setting. The hoard of words, the available resources of verbalization were essentially in paternal-masculine hands in the mixed familial situation; this same hoard could, as it were, be purloined and expended wastefully when women conversed among themselves and privily. The *salon*, as it begins during the seventeenth century, exactly defined a neutral ground: one on which men and certain elect women (such election being, however, ambiguous, in that it pointed to the blue-stocking, to the *frondeuse*, or to the 'emancipated' female) could claim and exercise equal rights of verbal instigation and response. The appeal for such rights is made poignant in *The Taming of the Shrew*, IV, iii, when Kate says:

> Why sir I trust I may have leave to speake,
> And speake I will. I am no childe, no babe,
> Your betters have indur'd me say my minde,
> And if you cannot, best you stop your eares,
> My tongue will tell the anger of my heart,
> Or else my heart concealing it will breake,
> And rather than it shall, I will be free,
> Even to the uttermost as I please in words.

The restriction here is subtle: the sole freedom possible to women in the classic order of familial-social primacies is, precisely, *in words*. But even Shakespeare, in terms charged with valuations of reciprocal speech-rights as old as the Pauline epistles, seems to give authority to Kate's final capitulation. And this capitulation once more underlines the dialectic of speech:

> Come, come, you froward and unable wormes,
> My minde hath bin as bigge as one of yours,
> My heart as great, my reason haplie more,
> To bandie word for word, and frowne for frowne;
> But now I see our Launces are but strawes . . .

In *The Silent Woman,* Shakespeare's contemporary, Ben Jonson, drastically conjoins suggestions of sexual and verbal incontinence: 'She is like a conduit-pipe that will gush out with more force when she opens again.'

What is unmistakable is the general sense of the compression of speech-energies in women by virtue of masculine-imposed criteria of decorum. Such compression must be equilibrated by compensatory modes of release ('or else my heart concealing it will break'). It is, therefore, more than probable that the sum of utterance in the lives of women, notably of educated women, during the sixteenth and seventeenth centuries and almost until the partial collapse of the *ancien régime* of familial hierarchies in the late eighteenth century, was unequally divided between audible speech and various modes of self-address. Besides expending words on one another, with an inflationary abandon which men suspected and satirized, women were necessarily liberal of speech to themselves. But they also availed themselves of a second instrument of inaudible eloquence: the letter. Here, again, statistics are either roughly conjectural or fail us altogether. But the collation of evidence from direct witness, from personal memoirs, from the importance which education and prescriptive works on gentility and right conduct attribute to the epistolary arts, together with what survives of correspondence, points to a 'golden age' of letter-writing from the rise of feminine literacy during the latter sixteenth century to a period roughly preceding the First World War. And there is every reason to believe that in the totality of epistolary production and exchange, the feminine component was major. To a marked degree, the personal letter represented the most ready and acceptable guise in which women could act politically, socially, psychologically on society at large. The private escritoire, be it in the life of Mme de Sévigné or in that of any female character in the novels of Jane Austen, is the privileged locus of the linguistic industry and verbal dissemination of women. But in composing a letter one speaks first and foremost to oneself (nothing is more significant of the verbal destitution of the servile classes, particularly in small-town and rural circumstances, than the compelled resort to public letter-writers and their set formulas on even the most spontaneous, intimate occasions of erotic appeal or family sorrow). Thus the immense current of 'lettered discourse' embodies and represents, at only one remove, the concomitant richness of inner speech. The letters of the classic age are soliloquies *á deux*.

It is a sociological commonplace that ours is not or no longer a letter-writing culture. This observation does not bear on quantity (consider the plethora of administrative, commercial, bureaucratic mail), but on function and quality. An ancillary and complex factor is that of the decline in hand-writing. In ways which are not clearly analysable, the temporal and formative relations of hand-writing to inner speech are more harmonically co-ordinate and immediate than are those of impersonal mechanical transcription such as that of the typewriter. The silences, the quasi-ritual privacies which accompanied the constant and voluminous production of epistolary acts in former times are no longer a current part of personal usage. The modern personal letter is, except in special cases which are themselves often imitative of an archaic motion, ephemeral. An entire register of narrative, introspective, confessional, commemorative notation and articulation, of which the epistolary novel which extends from the late Renaissance through *Pamela* and *La Nouvelle Héloïse* the whole way to Dostoevsky's *Poor Folk* is the outward manifestation, has lapsed from normal awareness. It has been widely argued that the telephone call has replaced the personal written missive. Where one formerly wrote a letter, by hand, one now makes a telephone call. Quantitative studies, particularly with regard to the United States, show that in the total aggregate of telephone-speech of a personal category, the feminine component is paramount. Nor can there be any doubt as to the linguistic and gestural wealth and complication of the resultant communicative act. Investigations of the relevant range of volume, pitch, stress, speed and idiomatic adjustments indicate that there is a 'telephone language' with its own distinctive features and semiotic context (there are women who make up or dress before telephoning). The telephone has complex functions in courtship and sexual role-playing. It helps to codify the linguistic devices of reciprocal identification, acceptance or refusal within and between peer and age-groups. But its relations to inner language and to the furnishings of silence which encompass inner language differ radically from those of the personal letter. Though this cannot be proved, the intuitive supposition is worth putting forward that the crucial distinction is one of time sequence. There is, especially in the case of hand-writing, a definite time-lapse between internalized enunciation — the *pre-scriptive* procedure of sentence or phrase-construction — and the externalizing movement of the hand. In the swift reciprocities of a telephone conversation, the temporalities of interior-exterior transfer are probably much more rapid and immediate. There may be an internalized rehearsal of reply by the listener (he is speaking his rejoinder to himself while listening to the voice of the caller); or there may be, particularly where teenage or feminine virtuosi of the medium are concerned, a near-abolition of the pre-scriptive plane. The language-stream is rapid, unmediated and semantically provisional — this is to say that meaning can at every moment be recalled, modulated, subverted by intonation. To anticipate the general finding of this essay, the personal letter in its classic phase cultivates and refines the inventory of inner discourse, whereas the telephone conversation consumes and vacates the reserves of inwardness (the telephone monologue, such as certain playwrights have used it for either tragic-solipsistic or comic purposes, would represent a problematic, fascinating intermediary between classic and modern types of self-expression).

The interactions of language and sexuality constitute one of the essential dynamics in the human condition. The plane of being on which these interactions occur is at once so vital and so complex that it negates the ordinary differentiations made between the psychological and the somatic, the spiritual and the neurochemical. The cardinal notion is that of a 'script'.[1] At any given instant, the composite of sexual behaviour is made up of an entire spectrum of determinants: there are implicit or explicit social conventions which will help to shape even the most private, seemingly instinctive performance; there are physiological constants, but these too seem to have their historicity and their social-psychological variants; there are superstructures of expectation, fantasy, moral coding which precede, envelope and classify the existential data. Together these form the script within or against which men and women enact their sexualities. In this script, the speech-components are pervasive and penetrating. A voluminous mythology, much of it verbally formulated and transmitted, precedes the fulfilment of homo- or heterosexual impulses. The scenario of excitement which stimulates and focuses the libido is, to a large extent, verbal, and there is every reason to suppose that there are structural analogies between and interactions of onanism and unvoiced soliloquy (onanism is a mode of autistic address). It is the sexual and the scatological in close contiguity, love having 'pitched its mansion in the house of excrement', which energize a substantial portion of taboo, underground and argotic parlance. It is, very likely, one of the more sensitive markers of the differentiations in the speech patterns of social classes, that this portion was, traditionally, externalized by the lower and internalized by the more privileged strata of the community. So close and mutually informing are the relations between sexuality and language, that certain social anthropologists categorize both as being branches of an encompassing semantic. The fundamental possibilities of sexual relations together with the concomitant prohibitions (incest) would have developed inseparably from the terminological and

[1] Cf. J.Gagnon, *Human Sexualities* (New York, 1977).

grammatical means of requisite designation (the exchange of words and that of women constitute analogous grammars, through them social consciousness is made articulate).

We know little of the history of successive sexual scripts. Evidence is suspect just because it is evidence — so much of the critical material being, almost by definition, private and even subconscious. Were middle-class young women in the nineteenth century as ignorant of sexual terminology and facts as romantic and Victorian homilies, novels, memoirs would have us believe? Is it conceivable, as some social psychologists have maintained, that female orgasm is itself a relatively late, historically-coded phenomenon, brought on not by inevitable physiology but by the gradual development of 'neuro-sociological' (we lack the proper term of compaction) expectations and awareness? To what degree is the relative distribution of sexual discourse between private and public, between socially-licit and clandestine, between genteel and argotic, a reliable guide to the study of erotic behaviour? At best, one proceeds tentatively.

For reasons which may be related to the new modes of domestic hygiene, to the contraction and economic formalization of the 'nuclear' family, to the fascinating and widespread reorientation of personal existence from the outside (the street, the common) to the interior of the house, the late sixteenth and early seventeenth centuries witness a sharp diminution in the area of permissible erotic speech and gesture. The Reformation is simultaneously a cause and beneficiary of this reduction. Rabelais, who still knew the old festive order, Montaigne and Shakespeare are the foremost observers of this modulation towards gestural and verbal constraint. Articulate bawdy becomes the ambiguous prerogative of the anarchic and servile elements in society. The official script is one of reticence or professed ignorance. The manufacture of pornography is so vital and inventive — notably during the eighteenth and nineteenth centuries — precisely because 'surface' discourse operates within a generally-enforced contract of denotative and inferential propriety. If the pragmatics and fantasy-life of sexuality are allowed overt linguistic expression, such expression is almost neutralized by the ritual of occasion: the military mess, the gentlemen's smoker, the bachelor's pre-nuptial *souper*. On open ground, between adult men and women, the script is one of silence or edulcorating paraphrase (the 'language of flowers', the lexicon of pastoral, the blushful idiom of the Valentine). Sensibility is expurgated, often masking the economic motives and brutalities of treatment which characterize the facts of married life (*Daniel Deronda, The Portrait of a Lady* are masterly documents of the dissociation between spoken and felt life, between roseate idiom and crass circumstance). When this script alters, it does so at surprising speed. Though any such dating is absurd, one would want to single out the tea-time in Bloomsbury when Lytton Strachey, observing a stain on Vanessa Bell's gown, threw out the immense single query: 'Semen?'

We are too near to the sources of this revolution in word and feeling, we are too intimately a part of it, to arrive at any confident aetiology. The breakdown of the high bourgeois-mercantile order in Europe, under stress of world war and economic crisis, is obviously a part of the cause. But more subterranean currents of revolt and positivity were at work. Among these psychoanalysis and the behavioural sciences are pre-eminent. We know now that psychoanalysis is, inescapably, a branch of applied linguistics. Freud, and Lacan after him, are 'meta-linguists', claiming to elicit the true meaning of meaning. We need not be concerned here with the growing realization that the Freudian theory and *praxis* of semiology was founded on an absurdly restrictive material base: that of the speech-script, extreme literacy, allusive conventions of middle-class diction among Central Europeans (mainly women) in the brief period from the 1880s to the 1920s. Nor need we engage the problem of the therapeutic undecidability of the analytic process (when is analysis 'completed', in what way could a cure be verifiably defined?). The paramount fact remains: psychoanalysis, directly and through its saturation of the climate of educated discourse and imagining, has radically shifted certain speech-balances. Revelation, audible utterance, externalization of even the most inward intentionalities and occlusions, either to the analyst-auditor or to others in society, or to oneself, has been made an instrument and validation of authenticity ('frankness as never before', wrote Pound). Free association is a device exactly calculated to pierce the membrane between inner and outer speech, to deflect into the diagnostic light and echo-chamber the unpremeditated rush and shadows of self-colloquy. It is a Freudian postulate that the motor-energies and referential tactics of the inward speech thus externalized and glossed will be primarily sexual. Even though this postulate has been qualified or partly abandoned by subsequent analytic schools, its effects on the erotic-semantic script have been decisive. So far as middle-class usage is concerned, particularly in the United States, the taboos enforced since the Renaissance have been lifted. If anything, explicitness of sexual pronouncement carries with it positive markers of adult poise and candour. The media have led and reflected the way. Some four centures of assumed or explicit censorship have collapsed nearly overnight in the domain of printed texts, stage-plays, films and the entire gamut of mass media. It is not easy to suggest any class of linguistic material or depiction which would still be subject to effective inhibition. The newsstand, the sex-emporium and the art of the novel after the failed prosecution of *Lady Chatterley's Lover* in 1962 represent a profound innovation (or reversion) in the psychosomatic environment, in the spaces of feeling and expression in which we conduct our affairs or dreams.

The consequences for the history of inner speech are, most probably, those of a drastic reapportionment. This would be most dramatically so in the case of middle-class women, many of whom will have passed within a generation from zones of near-silence or total inwardness in respect of sexual language to a milieu or permissiveness and, indeed, of competitive display. But the change would be scarcely less marked in the experience of the middle-class adolescent, and of numerous adult males (especially those lacking experience in the army barrack). Words, phrases, carnal exactitudes which were formerly unvoiced or which were reserved, kept numinous and pristinely exciting for occasions of utter intimacy and initiation (the lover teaching the beloved certain expressions, asking him or her to repeat them in a litany of complete trust), are now loud from every page, film-screen and hoarding. The night-words are the jargon of morning and noon. The statistically-oriented investigation into sexual behaviour, from Havelock Ellis to Kinsey and Masters and Johnson, has brought with it a fundamental impetus to publication, to making public in the full sense of the term. No less than the psychoanalyst, though within an entirely different methodological framework, the sociological interviewer, the social worker, the marriage counsellor, the spokesman in group therapy, elicit and reward the emission, the detailed externalization of what was once inchoate and private.

These mutations in script and value, in sense and sensibility, are far too manifold to judge peremptorily. What is involved is the pivotal concept of the economy of self. This economy depends on the allocation of mental and nervous resources as between the private and the public, the interior and the exterior, the autonomous and the collectively-focused aspects of our being. It involves the complex equations of solitude and gregariousness, of silence and of noise which seem to regulate the 'turning', the *Stimmung* as Heidegger would say, of identity. In this economy, the relative densities of inner and outer discourse and the dialectics of tension between these densities, play a significant part. Unquestionably, the proportions have altered massively, and in favour of the outside.

The receptor of the interior vocative can be one of the multitudinous fictions of the self: 'conscience', the 'sardonic narker', the 'empathic witness', 'the encourager', or any of a great range of accomplice or monitory personae (in the Thai language there is a special pronoun used when addressing oneself). It can be a presence drawn from either the living or the dead, or a composite of real and imagined figures. Customarily this lodger and listener inside will answer back. There is one significant exception in which the most intense of soliloquies and unvoiced speech-currents can assume a dialectical structure: the address of the self to God, whether it be in the mode of prayer, meditation or report. Except in the case of the illuminate and the mystic, no articulate reply is expected. But the implicit discourse is not unfocused, it is not freely associational as in the therapy situation. On the contrary, it is highly structured and historically coded. Unvoiced invocation to the deity is, presumably, a primal and universal element in all religious experience. But in the history of religions, as in that of language itself, there have been variations of stress as between externalized collective utterance and the inaudible colloquy of the individual and the numinous presence. The energies of domesticity (the turn towards and into the private room), the emphasis on individuation, the notion of psychic resources as being a capital worth amassing and investing prudentially, mark the movements of religious reform and the concurrent emergence of the modern middle classes during the sixteenth and, especially, during the seventeenth centuries. The seventeenth century can be documented as having been the classic period of inward religious address. We cannot dissociate virtuoso performances of sustained inward concentration such as the meditations of Pascal, the analytic introspections of Descartes or the monologues of ecstasy in St.John of the Cross, from a much wider executive form and practice. Within a mould of silence and privacy, the sensibility of the seventeenth century, in both its Reformation and Counter-Reformation guise, trained itself to achieve extraordinary intensities, durations and translucencies of autonomous, unspoken eloquence. This training has its deliberate pedagogic aspects. There is a considerable literature consisting of manuals of meditation, of progressively more arduous and prolonged exercises in silent concentration and exact focus. Baruzzi's magisterial study shows how the transcendent flights of ecstatic immediacy in St.John of the Cross, the augment of mortal speech into the 'grammar of light' before God, are generated by strict, perfectly rational drills and disciplines.[1] The exercises prescribed by Ignatius of Loyola aim to make of the wilful and disseminated bursts and eddies of interior speech a sharply-vectored, unwavering thrust. The analogy would be that of a laser beam so rigorously directed to the object of meditation — a sentence in a text, an iconic presentment of the saintly or divine presence, some precise feature of the Deity — as to allow no scatter. The spaces of introspective notice are to be cleansed of all except the chosen target. Such elimination of interference, of the phenomena of scatter and waste which characterize the normal streams of consciousness can only be achieved by severe training and conscription of will. Where it is accom-

[1] Jean Baruzzi, *Saint Jean de la Croix et le problème de l'expérience mystique* (Paris, 1924).

plished, there occurs that phenomenological reduction to pure apprehension, to absolute grasp (Husserl's phenomeno-logical exercises are explicitly related to the disciplines of Cartesian meditation) which enables the individual to engage in an authentic 'dialogue of one', between 'self and soul' as the baroque often phrases it, between self and God.

Linguistically, this mode of address is paradoxically public. Though stringently private and solitary in its setting, and solipsistic in its psychological means, the internalized rhetoric of the mystic, of the mediator, of the Puritan ponderer on scripture is precisely that: a rhetoric. We know from the exercises proposed for purposes of training as well as from the numerous testimonials of 'inner pilgrimage' (of which Bunyan's is exceptional only in regard to narrative richness) that inner discourse has its tropes, its topics, its taxonomies of pathos, no less than does voiced address and eloquence. The ultimate intimacies of the speaking ego, the self in its final nakedness, are semantically formal. There is, so far as word and syntax go, a confessional propriety, a decorum *in extremis* which distinguishes the acceptable styles of invoca-tion and self-analysis from the anarchic, vainglorious falsities of unmediated discourse indulged in by 'enthusiasts' of every breed (the Ranters, the babblers in Adamic tongues). In his chamber the silent soliloquist with and towards God, is soberly attired; his 'privity' aims at awesome communion. His unvoiced idiom, too, is garbed. It has, even in 'the spirit's lamentation', its logical armature which, notably in the reformed and Puritan worlds, was that taught by Ramus's *Dialectic*.

Again, quantification is impossible. One knows that in monastic orders and during periods of secular retreat, such as were widely practised throughout the sixteenth and seven-teenth centuries, silence and its accompaniment of internal exegetic, examinatory or meditative speech predominated.

One has grounds for supposing that the weight of quiet in the Calvinist, Puritan and Pietist households and the consequent inflection towards internalized modes of articulation, was considerable and may, in many instances, have tipped the balance of the day. This would also have been the case in the quasi-monastic conditions of Spanish courtly and genteel existence (of which the exercises of Loyola seem to have been a close reflection). The Pauline injunction to women's silence *in ecclesia* may have been matched by the sparsities of speech of the Puritan *pater familias* and the notorious taciturnity of the *hidalgo* (both strategies are ironized in Shakespeare's Malvoglio). We do not have enough reliable evidence to tell. But what cannot be overemphasized is the effect of generations of schooled introspection, of self-probing discourse, on the subsequent development of modern literature and of the modern typologies of personality. If the numbing silences of Scottish, Victorian and Lutheran Sundays are a direct legacy of seventeenth-century linguistic autism, so are the modern novel and the lyric of self-revelation. With the very gradual decline of formal religiosity in common life or, more exactly, with the partial metamorphoses of this religiosity into more generally 'humanistic' and worldly configurations of feeling, came a shift in the focus of self-address. Throughout the later seventeenth century we find a deepening fascination with the complexities of the ego, complexities not to be disciplined or even negated in the interest of immediacies of religious encounter, but on the contrary to be mapped and cultivated for their own sake. The prose novel, whose beginnings are so characteristically those of the fantasy-journey or of the epistolary dialogue, is the product of this fascination. And many of its early triumphs, such as the fictions of Rousseau, of Jane Austen, of the Brontës, directly embody the techniques and rhetorical conventions developed in previous periods of religious-ethical introspection and confessional notation. Concomitantly and against express prohibition (the reading of fiction on the Sabbath being deemed, in protestant households, a direct breach of the divine compact, almost to our own day), the novel takes over those functions and instrumentalities of analysis, of moral-psychological mapping and discrimination, of silent converse, which were once the staple of the sermon, of the exegetical tract, of the manual of spiritual exercises. It is the genius of the Joycean interior monologue to make articulate within itself the entire moral and technical history of self-discourse, and it is no accident that Joyce works out his idiom with specific reference to Jesuitical procedures of meditational, unvoiced elocution.

The concentration on what Gerard Manley Hopkins called 'inscape' found transcription into another textual register even more immediate to the pulse of inner speech than is the novel. We have no count of the millions, of the tens of millions of words set down by men and women in private diaries and journals during the golden age of the genre, from the early seventeenth century to the years just after the First World War (this terminal date is bound to be conjectural). The implicit or explicit, subconscious or conscious orders of motivation, of receptive intention can vary the whole way from a journal such as that of the Goncourts, conceived to be read by the world at large 'one day', to the self-dramatizing privacies of diaries set down in cipher. The styles of address, of titular location between writer and reader exhibit the same variousness. Dorothy Wordsworth's journals are brilliant trials of perception and notation, endeavours of the transported, sensorily-sharpened self to submit to the reflecting and critical ego the data of ecstatic experience. The inward dialogue in Henry James is pursued between the restive, recalcitrant persona of the baffled or disenchanted craftsman, often imaged as *mon vieux*, and the super-id, as it were, of moral-aesthetic commitment and material compulsion. Kafka's diaries are part of an extremely complex, almost pathological discipline of self-distancing, of self-estrangement, in which the man and the writer construe between themselves those modes of haunted impersonality which organize Kafka's parables and tales. The massive journals kept by Cosima Wagner are a ritual self-dedication to the master's arduous service, yet also an ambiguous ritual in that they presume an unknown but sympathetic reader who will, in future, bear witness to the depth of the writer's sacrifice, to the expense of spirit in abnegation. All these are public peaks of a literally incommensurable hidden industry. When fully published, Amiel's mid-nineteenth century journal, almost certainly meant only for his own eyes, will run to some sixteen thousand closely-printed pages. The diaries of Virginia Woolf are reputed to comprise some twenty volumes. Wars, accident and social dislocation have certainly destroyed a mass of documentation; a comparable mass remains unpublished, in the family attic, in the bank-vault, in the never-looked at Regency or Victorian personal album with its marbled boards or tooled leather and clasps. Again, the role of women diarists in the total aggregate may well have been paramount. The young girl's journal, the often stylized mirror of guarded intimacies (whose exchange with that of the husband on or just before marriage constitutes so obvious a sexual-semantic equation) appears to have been a staple of genteel upbringing. It is in her most secret diary, as Balzac, George Eliot, Turgenev narrate, that the young wife and mother voices the epiphanies, disappointments or raw sorrow of her condition. Barred from public expression of political, ideological and psychological conviction or discovery, the intelligent woman in the *ancien régime* and nineteenth century makes her journal the forum, the training ground of the mind. The man, in turn, may confide to the trusteeship of his diaries material of an as yet socially inadmissible category, particularly in respect of sexual experience, whether actual or fictive (Michelet's intimate journals are a striking but by no means isolated case). The point is worth stressing: methodologically and in substance, much of what still passes for social history and for the scholarly reconstruction of the climate of sentiment, of the literacies of psychological awareness before Freud and modern 'emancipation' is, probably, inaccurate: it overlooks the sophistications of social-psychological insight and data contained in the fantsatically loquacious world of the diary. This is so especially of the analyses of dreams set down voluminously in this private mode.

Loquacity, copiousness and temporal duration characterize the idiolects of diary-writers. But here, as in the intimate records of self-correction, of the keeping of private accounts before God common to the seventeenth century (the massive diaries of Kierkegaard exactly mark the transition from the heuristic-meditational to the modern vein), the stream of speech is inward. The rhetorical structures are unvoiced, the acts of self-address are performed in silence (innumerable journals tell of the privileged nocturnal hours in which the writer turns from the tumult of the domestic or public day to the healing silences of the self). Once more, we are dealing with linguistic production whose lexical and grammatical conventions may closely mirror those of external, audible utterance — this is not always the case, as we know from coded diaries and from journals set down in partly infantile, partly 'made up' vocabularies — but whose statistical extent and intentionality belong to the shadow-side of discourse. And once again, separations by gender and social class seem to have been critical: the productivity of women in this sphere was probably preponderant, and that of the lower classes, even where individuals were technically literate, seems to have been very scant (the 'diary of the chambermaid' is, with very few known exceptions, a fiction of male erotic fantasy). Thus we find a distribution of discourse with a strongly internalizing factor.

It is impossible to say with any confidence whether or not the diary habit has declined generally. For what it is worth, it is one's impression that this is indeed so. The tempo of the middle-class day, the new licenses and positive valuation given to every kind of intimate 'publication' and self-expression, the decay of hand-writing — a phenomenon whose socio-psychological implications have been little explored — the complex but radical changes in the whole theory and *praxis* of privacy — all these point towards the gradual erosion of the diary medium. Great twentieth-century diaries, such as Gide's, are highly self-conscious, even archaicizing gestures (in Gide's case, reference to the Pascalian precedent is constant). The diaries of modern politicians and diplomats are, in fact, public papers which observe a convention of temporary discretion. Techniques of therapeutic externalization have essentially replaced the role of the diary in the conservation of interior poise, in the defusing of potentially contagious elements of fantasy-life and psychic suggestion. Here again, a covert but consequential alteration has taken place in the respective dimensions and authority of outer and inner speech.

One further aspect of this change needs mention. A hierarchical order, a classic social structure defines itself and articulates its power relations in reference to a shared syllabus of texts. These can, as in the case of republican Rome, be prophetic and juridical; they can, as in the Enlightenment, be stylistic and philosophical; the shared syllabus of the Victorian ruling caste is that of the Authorized Version, of certain Latin classics, notably Horace and Virgil, of the Book of Common Prayer and of the axis of national poetic genius as it runs from Shakespeare and Milton through Gray to Tennyson. But in each case, the crucial device is that of a consensual echo formed by generally available citation from, allusion to, inference of, one or more of the canonic texts. This device depends, in large part, on a mnemonic base. We have alluded to the *ars memoriae* used by late medieval and Renaissance disciplines in the mental ordering and retention of knowledge. It can be said that the education of the European lettered men and women, particularly of men, from the grammar and monastic schools of the sixteenth century, through the lycées, *gymnasia* and public schools of the nineteenth century, almost to the present, was also an *ars memoriae*. In it, learning *by heart* (an idiom worth thinking about) was the dominant method and aim. The almost implausible mnemonic feats of a young Macaulay, who knew a fair measure of the Western classics by heart before entering university, have biographical notoriety. But something approaching this degree of trained recall was, in fact, the norm of middle-class political and intellectual literacy. Recall by heart of extensive tracts of classical verse and biblical narrative or prophecy was the assumed guarantor of civil, intellectual and even private exchange. The profound effects of this training and usage of memory on the architecture of sensibility and on the organization of speech have never been investigated adequately. But they were, quite obviously, considerable. To take only the English case, we know from diaries, journals, private memoirs, correspondence and reports of conversation, how deeply the habits of perception and reference drawn from Horace or Virgil, from Scripture or Shakespeare, reached into the life and utterance of the mind. Again and again, though the diarist or speaker may be unconscious of the fact, apparently native and unpremeditated testimonies of personal feeling take on a cononic guise (domesticity and old age are voiced in the manner of Horace or Catullus, men wax jealous to the cadence of Othello; when the Brontës or George Eliot record their innermost tribulations and resolutions they do so, often unawares, in the precise idiom of Ecclesiastes, the Psalms or the Pauline epistles). In short: inner consciousness and speech are made dense with, are charged by, the specific imprint of literacy on remembrance (and it is on this referential literacy, as it reaches to the very roots of the subconscious, that so much of Freudian decoding relies).

Nowhere has the change in the values and practices of Western middle-class culture been more readily observable. Progressive and populist ideals of education can nearly be defined by virtue of their opposition to 'learning by heart'. The electronically-expressed and inventoried 'information explosion' has been such as to make the mnemonic means of the ordinary brain inadequate and unreliable. There is no longer, moreover, a widely-agreed canon of exemplary texts, dates or recognitions. Mappings of what it is that a man or woman must know, must know well enough to call at once to mind to refer to, imply manifestly or cite, are now as diverse and reciprocally polemic as are ideologies or ethnic-political identifications. Even where vestiges of such an agreed syllabus and echo-repertoire exist, the changes in the structures of leisure and attention, the magnified exposure of individual attention to the information-avalanche and syn-chronic immediacies of the media, leave little time and little natural space for the cultivation of memory. In many politically-ecumenical and technologically-oriented school systems, notably in the United States, the education of the young is planned amnesia (for reasons of censorship, of vital oral tradition, and of the relatively backward state of the electronic mass-media, the Soviet Union and eastern Europe represent a challenging exception; that which is known by heart, from literature, from history, plays a crucial part in the survival of individual and social integrity). In the West, we carry far less inner ballast than did the literate caste, the shapers of spirit and of speech, in preceding generations. Here again, the material and moral desolation of the First World War and its aftermath seem to mark a watershed.

To summarize: the totality of human linguistic production, the sum of all significant lexical and syntactic units generated by human beings, can be divided into two portions: audible and inaudible, voiced and unvoiced. The unvoiced or internal components of speech span a wide arc: all the way from the subliminal flotsam of word or sentence-fragments which, presumably, are a perpetual current or currency of every phenomenology of consciousness, sleeping and waking, to the highly-defined, focused and realized articulacy of the silent recitation of a learned text or of the taut analytic moves in a disciplined act of meditation. Quantitatively, there is every reason to believe that we speak inside and to ourselves more than we speak outward and to anyone else. Qualitatively, these manifest modes of self-address may enact absolutely primary and indispensable functions of identity; they test and verify our 'being there'. Taken together, internal and external discourse constitute the economy of existence, of our presentness, in a way which philosophers, from Heraclitus to Heidegger, have characterized as quintessentially human.

This paper has suggested that there is a history, a morphology, a rhetoric of inner speech as there is of outer. The relationships of internal language to the environment are dialectical, precisely as are those of voiced utterance; they help to create the world of experience and, at the same time, reflect it. The very notion of history entails that of change. In the case of inward speech, this change can be two-fold: the relative proportions of inner and outer address within the semantic whole can alter, and there can be transformations in the functions and composition of the internalized mode. As would be the case in any dynamic composite, these two sorts of change will tend to be congruent. Function and structure will alter with proportion. But the point needs refinement: the total quantity of internal speech acts, their mean rate and frequency may well be a constant of the entropy of the psyche. What has changed will be the relative intensity and significance of these acts in proportion to outward discourse, and their morphology.

There is evidence that such a change has taken place between the late sixteenth and seventeenth centuries, which may have been the classic age of soliloquy, and the speech-sensibility of the present. Certain absolutely key aspects of the relative distribution of psychological and social identity and value as between private and public, unvoiced and declared, religious and secular, have been more or less drastically modified. The contribution of women, of the young, of the economically and socially less advantaged levels of the community to the aggregate of enunciation, has sharply increased. Seminal areas of self-enclosure, of a social contract of mutually-agreed taciturnity, on sex, on the life of fantasy and nervous tension, but also on monetary affairs (the taboo on the discussion of one's earnings or real wealth), have been opened up to examination and avowal. Today, the stress is on 'saying all', on telling 'how it is', in explicit rebuttal to what are regarded as archaic, class-determined, uptight atavisms of censorship and decorum. Concurrently, there has been a marked decline in those techniques of concentrated linguistic internality which went with religious meditation, methodical introspection and learning by heart (it is striking to what extent the pseudo-oriental practices of meditation now in vogue in the West, and among the children of a pulverized middle-class, aim at ideals of verbal minimalism, of image rather than word, of sonorous vacancy; in current sensibility this part of Asia is remote from the scholastic nicety and discursive wealth of Cartesian, Pascalian or Kierkegaardian descent into the self). The approved loquacities of psychoanalysis, of mundane confession, as they are practised in modern therapy, in modern literature, in competitive gregariousness and on the media, go directly counter to the ideals of communicative reticence or autonomy represented by the private letter, diary or journal. The telephone consumes, with utter prodigality, raw materials of language of which a major portion was once allocated to internal use or to the modulated inwardness of the private, silently conceived written correspondence. One is tempted to conclude that where much more is, in fact, being heard, less is being said.

The concept of an economy of and within personal identity is teleological, this is to say that it implies aims of equilibrium. The creative well-being of an organic system depends on intricate balance between stimulus and repose, between use and recuperation. This balance, in turn, derives from adjustments between inner and outer environment. Language constitutes both in the most immediate and dynamic sense. It is the pulse and skin of conscious being. It draws its energies from interactions of silence and noise, of emission and retention, of containment and disclosure, far more complex and topologically ingenious than any we can imagine, let alone map. Rudimentary as they are, our diagnoses of autism, of aphasia, of speech disorders that range from extreme inhibition to ungoverned flow, tell us that these interactions are acutely vulnerable. Arguably, the most crucial of these reciprocities is that between outer and inner discourse, between the inter-personal and intra-personal dimensions in the linguistic whole. If this is so, a change of relative weight is one that would affect the personality of the individual and his stance in the world.

This essay has put forward the thought (the variousness and ambiguous tenor of the evidence are such as to allow no categorical or conclusive formulation) that the shift in the balance of discourse since the seventeenth century has been *outward*. There would seem to have been a concomitant impoverishment in the articulate means of the inward self. We have lost a considerable measure of control over the fertile ground of silence. Expending so much more of our 'speech-selves', we have less in reserve. In a sense that fully allows the play on meaning, the centre of gravity has been displaced, and we bend outward, mundanely, from the roots of our being. One might almost define the decline of a classic value-structure, as felt in the Renaissance and seventeenth century, and active still among the literate until the great crises of world war and social revolution, as being a shift from an internalized to a voiced convention of personality and utterance. Whether it is this shift, rather than any political-economic crises, that underlies the widely-debated but little understood phenomena of anomie, of alienation, of anarchy of feeling and gesture in the current situation, is a question worth raising.

5

Eros and Idiom

1975

In Chapter XI of Book III of *Emma* the heroine is shocked into a realization of her own condition of feeling:

> Harriet was standing at one of the windows. Emma turned round to look at her in consternation, and hastily said,
>
> 'Have you any idea of Mr.Knightley's returning your affection?'
>
> 'Yes,' replied Harriet modestly, but not fearfully—'I must say that I have.'
>
> Emma's eyes were instantly withdrawn; and she sat silently meditating, in a fixed attitude, for a few minutes. A few minutes were sufficient for making her acquainted with her own heart. A mind like hers, once opening to suspicion, made rapid progress. She touched—she admitted—she acknowledged the whole truth. Why was it so much worse that Harriet should be in love with Mr.Knightley, than with Frank Churchill? Why was the evil so dreadfully increased by Harriet's having some hope of a return? It darted through her, with the speed of an arrow, that Mr.Knightley must marry no one but herself!

The economy of the passage is all. This economy is the immediate product of a large confidence, of a community of response between Jane Austen and her material and the novelist and her readers. Such community expresses itself in a prose which is, structurally, a shorthand. The words used by the novelist draw on public energies, on areas of meaning and implication which may be wide but whose reach of admissible reference is determined. The idiomatic carries a general charge of required significance. Metaphors are relatively infrequent or when they appear they do so in a condition of eroded vitality. Another way of saying that a language can move richly while 'on the surface' is to say that *Emma* was written in a time, in a moment of culture, in which style and convention were close.

A closeness of this kind usually has behind it a strong literary manner now attenuated and become a part of current speech. Below the concise ease of Emma's self-recognition runs the current, once sharply stylized, of Restoration comedy. It is the established specificity of the terminology of manner and feeling in Restoration comedy and the sentimental novel of the late eighteenth century that enables Jane Austen to proceed with speed and confident exactitude. There is no need of shading or of the vital indeterminacies of the modern tone. *Heart* and *mind* have their own determined valuations in a vocabulary of consciousness no doubt complex and particular in its historical roots but, so far as the novelist is concerned, now available for direct, unencumbered use. The 'evil so dreadfully increased' carries considerable intensity, but it is subverted, to the precise measure of irony required, by the fact that it belongs to an idiom conventionally, fictionally heightened into imperfect gravity. There is no mistaking the gestures, hence no need of elaboration or localized stress. The turn in consternation, the eyes instantly withdrawn, Emma's fixity, are parts of a code of significant manners as declaratory in their simplicity, in their lack of visual rhetoric, as is her diction. And it is precisely the triumph of a mastered conventionality to make its own individual, richly felt point in the most public of ways: that arrow of love darting through Emma. Nothing could be more deliberately worn, more void of its initial, long-forgotten metaphoric vivacity. The shaft of love piercing the unwilling or unknowing maiden's heart had, long before *Emma*, lost even the salience of a *cliché*. Yet Jane Austen can afford this dead turn and can make it active. The banality of the image qualifies — a qualification urged throughout the novel — the genuine authority and hurt of Emma Woodhouse's feelings. Her vulnerabilities are real but bounded, which defining limitation is beautifully enforced by the very turn of the phrase: 'Mr.Knightley must marry no one but herself!' The imperious note, Emma's placing of herself at the centre, the mere setting of the last word, restore to self-confidence, and restore to our own sense of a necessary if gentle irony, the figure of the young woman woken to love. Where conventions of expressive form are so stable and so explicitly associative of writer to reader, syntax comes fully into its own.

The active life of conventionality is notable, principally, in Jane Austen's handling of the implicit sexual material. So direct yet unobtrusively public is the available idiom that we almost overlook the raw facts of the situation: two women in love and necessarily rival. Both the allusion to Frank Churchill and the predatory, if comic, pulse of the last sentence, sharpen the edge of feeling. It is men and women who are in play and the gamut of possibilities between them from seduction to marriage. Emma is transformed body and soul, within the limitations of crisis allowed by Jane Austen. A few moments later Miss Woodhouse is at the edge of her own sense of being: 'ashamed of every sensation but the one revealed to her — her affection for Mr.Knightley. — Every other part of her mind was disgusting.' Yet the sexual turbulence, the implications of action that flow from the muted encounter of Emma and Harriet, cannot, need not be articulated. They are inside the narrative, not in the sense of impulse hidden or unconscious, but as an area of understood meaning so intelligently faced, so publicly acquiesced in — the novelist and her reader having, as it were, negotiated a treaty of mutual intent — that there is no need of localizing articulation. Such a pact, in reference to sexuality, is the underlying condition of Jane Austen's art. Without it she could not proceed as swiftly and with as confidently limited a completeness as she does. The 'negotiation' of that *entente* is a long story. It involves the middle-class rejection of the open eroticism — open in the sense of being pictorial, punning, metaphorically unstable — of Restoration comedy, while at the same time absorbing much of that eroticism into senti-mental fiction. In Samuel Richardson eroticism shifts from solicitation to spectacle; a distance of condescension and socially informed sentiment, adroitly varied by the novelist, intervenes between the world of the fiction and that of the reader. Jane Austen is heir to that 'distancing', although in her what had been in *Clarissa* a zone of prurience is now firm, neutral ground. But the most relevant fact is that Jane Austen's conventionality, free and intelligent as it strikes us, was already a rearguard action, an attempt to transmit to a new, splintered society standards, manners of judgment founded in the culture of the age of Johnson and Cowper. By the time of *Mansfield Park* and *Emma* the erotic imagination had broken free on at least two principal lines: in the trashy but often cunningly stylized and 'psychologically under-pinned' sexuality of the Gothic novel, and in the lyric con-creteness of Romantic poetry. Sixteen years before *Emma*, in the Preface to the *Lyrical Ballads*, William Wordsworth had firmly related 'the sexual appetite' to 'the great spring of the activity of our minds'. And one need but glance at the 'Lucy' poems to realize how far Wordsworth's terminology had advanced toward a complex, disturbingly penetrative use of sexual symbolism. In their treatment of the relations of feeling and desire between men and women, the novels of Jane Austen represent a rearguard action. They succeed through sheer force of serenity (a serenity obviously related to their total refusal of contemporaneous politics and history). But such leisured progress on a tightrope could not be performed again. In Jane Austen sex is, essentially, gender. The terms were soon to be reversed.

But neither as rapidly nor as generally as might have been expected. Jane Austen's contract had looked to the past. It was based on minority values and a theory of formal expression. The erotic reticence or erosive conventionality of the English novelists of the mid-century had broader motives. The novel had become the principal currency of middle-class feeling with its expectations of entertainment, of unobtrusive instruction, and, above all, of emotional and intellectual 'familiarity'. Both connotations, intimacy and familial tone, are important. The Victorian novel-reader wished to be at home in the world of his reading and demanded that those in his sitting-room be a party to his pleasures. Publishers, home-libraries, periodicals, an entire industry of allowed sensibility, flourished in response to well-established canons of imaginative temperance and domesticity. Economically this helped bring on a formidable expansion of serious if 'middle-brow' literacy. Artistically it necessitated a series of concessions or evasive tactics on the part of the novelists. In no one did necessary concession and bias of temper unite more coherently than in Dickens. His genius and the representative stature he achieved were in large part the result of a vital accord between the taste of the public and Dickens's profound sympathy with that taste.

The complicated energies released in Dickens's work pose many problems. None is more arresting than the fact that no other writer of comparable stature, of even related imaginative multiplicity in any modern literature, has ever been so innocent of stated adult sexuality. To say that this innocence has made of Dickens a classic for children or, more accurately, a classic whom adults re-read in a special ambience of remembered trust (we cannot so re-read *Gulliver's Travels*), is merely to point to an obvious consequence. Dickens's refusal of adult sexuality left clear marks. The symbolic vehemence and scarcely mastered crudity of melodrama in *Bleak House* and *Great Expectations* suggest a subterranean pressure of erotic recognition. The curious flashes of cruelty and hysteria notable as early as the 'black tales' in *Pickwick Papers* persist; they give to *Little Dorrit* much of its disturbing strength. But more often and, so far as Dickens's enormous readership was concerned, more characteristically, the absence of the erotic produced varieties of sentimentality. Dickens created a garden for fallen man, a nursery world from which middle-class optimism and bustle have, temporarily at least, banished the serpent. The Dora-David-Agnes relationship in *David Copperfield* is as deliberate a pastoral as any to be found in the Renaissance trope of the garden of love. It relegates the values of adult sexuality to the 'innocent' eroticism of the child (innocent before Freud). Dickens touches with sure instinct on a chord vibrant even in severe Protestantism: the resistance of the imagination to the thought that children too have been mined by original sin. In *The Turn of the Screw*, Henry James was to create a parody, deliberately sexual in focus, of Dickens's 'juvenal-pastoral'.

Dickens's achievement is formidable, but not all could so readily pay the price. Thackeray's relations with his middle-class audience and the latter's criteria of sexual tameness were unsteady and, at moments, waspish. His recourse, both emotional and strategic, to the eighteenth century points directly towards a lost candour and robustness in the erotic. Hence the famous complaint in the Preface to *Pendennis* that the novelist must drape masculinity and give 'a certain conventional simper' to his depiction of man, that no one since Fielding had been allowed to show man whole. Thackeray's malaise is evident in the flawed genius of *Vanity Fair*. Becky Sharp's career, set down by the novelist in precise contemporaneity with Marx's *Communist Manifesto*, illustrates what is probably the foremost insight of the modern novel: the interweaving, the symbolic and structural interchange between economic and sexual relations. It develops Balzac's recognition that class, sex, and money are expressions of more essential, underlying power relations. But, as often in Thackeray, the lack of available frankness induces a satirical, mock-ceremonious tone. Compelled to observe 'family manners' which are at odds with the abrasive candour of his perceptions, Thackeray writes tangentially; being less than 'Man' his personages accept all too easily the designation of puppets.

The case most difficult to account for in terms of middle-class taste and professional response is, of course, that of the Brontës. The depth of sexual commitment in *Wuthering Heights* is disguised or rather stylized by a brilliant recourse to already obsolete Gothic counters. *Jane Eyre* aroused hostility by its assumption of sexual readiness – poised, asking for mature arousal – in a 'decent' woman. But here also an intense stylization occurs. We may observe, in the encounters of the heroine and Rochester, how sexuality is made elemental, how a vocabulary of feverish grandeur effaces specific eroticism. In Charlotte Brontë, as in Lucretius, there is the vision of a world totally, therefore in the last analysis innocently, guiltlessly, informed by desire. Precisely because it is a lesser work, *Villette* proved more indicative of future solutions. The pressure of erotic recollections is intense; but the narrative moves on a level of symbolic realism, of natural incidents symbolically ordered, which was to give prose fiction its full authority. From *Villette* it was but a step to the more confident art of George Eliot.

There are several reasons why *Middlemarch* is pre-eminent among English novels, why it exhibits a cumulative genius of persuasion which, almost inevitably, directs one to Tolstoy. One of the main causes is the quality and extent of George Eliot's information, the sheer pressure of knowledge, exact and imaginatively mastered, she brings to bear on every aspect of her material. It is this particular authority of the thoroughly *known* which gives to the novel – 'vast, swarming, deep-coloured, crowded with episodes', as Henry James termed it[1] — a firm pivot. We do not find before *Middlemarch* (and we scarcely find again in the subsequent history of the English novel) the erudition, the responsible learning dramatically imagined and conveyed, which make possible the treatment of Lydgate's medical work and ambitions in Chapter XV of Book II. The description of Reform Bill agitation and of the role of the new journalism in it — a role ironically yet understandingly located in the novelist's handling of Will Ladislaw — again draws its conviction from a body of knowledge personally gathered, wholly ordered, and in reach of feeling. This same authority informs George Eliot's presentation of the two principal sexual motifs in the book, the Dorothea-Casaubon fiasco and Lydgate's relationship to Rosamond.

The narrative of the Casaubon honeymoon, with its possible reference to the life of Mark Pattison, is so closely meshed that it is difficult to locate in any single passage the full tact and perception of the novelist. The city of Rome is made the direct symbolic counterpart of Dorothea's bewilderment. 'The past of a whole hemisphere seems moving in funeral procession with strange ancestral images and trophies gathered from afar. But this stupendous fragmentariness heightened the dream-like strangeness of her bridal life.' The very season informs against the obscurely woken young woman: 'autumn and winter seemed to go hand in hand like a happy aged couple one of whom would presently survive in chiller loneliness.' Working in this chapter (XX, Book II) at the tense limits of available concretenesss, George Eliot does resort to uneasy paraphrase: 'Forms both pale and glowing took possession of her young sense'; 'many souls in their young nudity are tumbled out among incongruities'. The uncharac-

---

[1] Henry James, 'The Novels of George Eliot', in *Views and Reviews* (London, 1908).

teristic baroque touch is deeply informative: the 'young nudity' is not primarily that of the soul, a point clarified, if any such clarification is required, by a constant reference to the statues and paintings seen by Dorothea. The 'incongruities' (and 'tumbled' is a beautifully betraying verb) are those of a brutal marital fiasco. But such is the density and strong pulse of the narrative that the local need for paraphrase, with its attendant risk of modish allegory, does not dim the precise, radical truth:

Now, since they had been in Rome, with all the depths of her emotion roused to tumultuous activity, and with life made a new problem by new elements, she had been becoming more and more aware, with a certain terror, that her mind was continually sliding into inward fits of anger and repulsion, or else into forlorn weariness.

The vocabulary remains 'chaste' in the precise Augustan sense of the word, the chastity being largely a matter of abstraction, of a generalized syntax. But the cumulative intensity of George Eliot's manner, her power to suggest a known particularity, make the full meaning of what she is saying unmistakable. When the physical touch does come, the effect is the more poignant: 'she had ardour enough for what was near, to have kissed Mr.Casaubon's coat-sleeve, or to have caressed his shoe-latchet.' The master-stroke, moreover, comes later, when the honeymoon is a sombre recollection. At the close of Chapter XXIX of Book III, Dorothea and Celia are talking of the latter's engagement to Sir James Chettam. Will Dodo be glad to see Sir James and hear him tell of his cottages?

'Of course I shall. How can you ask me?'
'Only I was afaid you would be getting so learned,' said Celia, regarding Mr.Casaubon's learning as a kind of damp which might in due time saturate a neighbouring body.

The image comes through with repellent force. It tells of sexual failure and revulsion. The contrasting note of sentimental fecundity in Celia and the cottages is delicately struck. The rich exactitude of physical implication is achieved through an exercise of narrative truth so complete, so spaciously laid out, that we do not resent or experience as dated the abstraction, the extreme reticence of George Eliot's idiom.

This idiom is, appropriately, somewhat different in the Lydgate-Rosamond strands of the novel. 'There is nothing more powerfully real than these scenes in all English fiction,' wrote Henry James,[1] 'and nothing certainly more *intelligent*.' That reality does not stem from naive verisimilitude. It is, at decisive moments, achieved by means essentially emblematic. As has been repeatedly noticed, Lydgate's courtship of Rosamond and the subsequent crises of their marriage are punctuated by a set of key images. An entire range of dramatic tones is expressed through Rosamond's 'fair long neck' and the submissions or angry turns it performs. A larger nakedness is set out in that 'exquisite nape which was shown in all its delicate curves' (Chapter LVIII, Book VI). The covert echoes of Eve and of the serpent with 'sleek enameled neck' enforce the gravity of Lydgate's fall. With a degree of control almost Shakespearean, in that it 'misses nothing', the novelist again focusses our attention on Rosamond's neck during the climactic meeting between Rosamond and Dorothea. But here the erotic values are suppressed and the statement is one of agonized candour; what we are directed to now is 'Rosamond's convulsed throat' (the careful imitation of Milton at the end of the chapter clinches the latent identification of Rosamond). Nor ought we to miss the confident, almost theatrical placing of symbolic props in the narrative of Lydgate's proposal (Chapter XXXI, Book III). Lydgate 'moved his whip and could say nothing.' Rosamond 'dropped her chain as if startled, and rose too, mechanically' ('as if' and 'mechanically' alert us to an inevitable artifice). 'When he

[1] *Ibid.*

rose he was very near to a lovely little face set on a fair long neck.' We cannot evade the serpentine note. Lydgate 'did not know where the chain went'; but in half an hour he leaves the house fettered, a man 'whose soul was not his own, but the woman's to whom he had bound himself'.

In what measure is George Eliot conscious of the associations she so exactly invokes, of the symbolic contents, to us so graphically Freudian, of that moving whip and broken chain? She does not need to be conscious of them in our sense of deliberate, 'publicly coded' significance. Her intellectual and psychological awareness is as complete as that of any twentieth-century novelist, as directly germane to the intended effect, but it has a different 'knowingness'. This difference is the key point.

George Eliot's perceptions of sexual feeling, the closeness of observation she brings to bear on erotic sensibility and conflict, yield nothing to that of the moderns. In most instances what passes for characteristic post-Freudian insight is, by comparison, shallow. But these perceptions and the free play of imaginative recognition are immensely in advance of, immensely more explicit than, the vocabulary available to a serious novelist of the 1870s. George Eliot knows more, far more, than she says or feels called upon to *say*; but that knowledge, precise, informed by a marvellous grasp of human particularity, gives to what is said an unmistakable authority, an energy of undeclared content felt, registered, though as it were unheard. Between the urgent wealth of felt life and the actual idiom of the novel there is a zone of silence, an area of conventional selection in which the novelist's responses — material, psychologically informed, canny as are any of the moderns — are translated into the temperance and conventional indirection of Victorian public speech. But it is just this distance, this close presence of the known but unstated, that gives to the novel its intensity, its matchless energy of

adult life. At every point in the treatment of Dorothea's
unsentimental education or of Lydgate's submission to
Rosamond, George Eliot's verbal reticence stands not for
thinness, for absence of radical intelligence, but on the
contrary for a nearness of unwasted resource. This reticence,
moreover, this deliberate tact, allow effects of sensibility
almost lost to modern fiction. The novelist treats both her
characters and her readers as complex beings; she would not
search out the last privacy of self. Hence her largesse of
imaginative acceptance. At the close of Book IV, the darkness
of the Casaubon marriage deepens into explicit night.
Dorothea watches her ailing husband coming upstairs, a light
in hand:

'Dorothea!' he said, with a gentle surprise in his tone, 'Were you
waiting for me?'

'Yes. I did not like to disturb you.'

'Come, my dear, come. You are young, and need not to extend your
life by watching.'

When the kind quiet melancholy of that speech fell on Dorothea's
ears, she felt something like the thankfulness that might well up in us if
we had narrowly escaped hurting a lamed creature. She put her hand
into her husband's, and they went along the broad corridor together.

The focus is steady and unswervingly honest: the image of
the 'lamed creature' carries all the relevant charge of frustra-
tion, of a relationship irreparably crippled (how much we
lose by our knowingness about the symbolic, almost lexical
equivalent between lameness and castration). But the wonder
of the thing lies in its generosity, in the realization unfolded
in Dorothea and the reader of Casaubon's human complication, of the claims which that complication can make on our
response. This brief nocturne, once again rounded with a
Miltonic echo, sets the art of George Eliot beside that of
Tolstoy. The authority of compassion is as controlling, as
humanizing here as it is in Tolstoy's treatment of Alexei

Karenin. But note how closely it depends on the reticence of the medium. It would be impossible for George Eliot to evoke this delicacy of response, this completeness of sympathy, had the ugliness, the rot of body and nerve in Dorothea's honeymoon and married life, been made verbally explicit. Chasteness of discourse acts not as a limitation but as a liberating privacy within which the characters can achieve the paradox of autonomous life.

The lag of permissible terminology behind perception, and the narrative poise it made necessary and possible, did not last. The formal conventions and social expectations involved were too manifold to be stable. Henry James's *The Portrait of a Lady* is at significant points a *reprise* of *Middlemarch*. But the intervening years, short as they were, and even more so James's own view[1] of *Middlemarch* as setting a limit 'to the development of the old-fashioned English novel,' have brought a difference. The treatment of the corroding marriage of Isabel Archer and Gilbert Osmond is indebted to the Dorothea-Casaubon theme; Florence and the chill discretion of fine art close on Isabel as Rome closed on Dorothea. The 'vivid flash of lightning' which at last brings Dorothea and Ladislaw together strikes again as Casper Goodwood embraces Mrs.Osmond. But the inwardness which James aims for, the explicit sophistication of psychological analysis, are such that a generalized, unworried vulgate is no longer adequate. The knowledge possessed by the novelist no longer underlines the narrative; it presses on it and insinuates into the writer's style a new consciousness of symbolism. In Henry James chasteness and reserve are deliberate means; we are meant to observe the strenuous tactics of exclusion. What is left out lies in ambush around the next corner. In the Jamesian novel or in such specific uses of 'mask' as James's ghostly tales, reticence about sexual matters is not a statement of felt life,

[1] *Ibid.*

but a subtle privation. Often the unsaid comes through with a kind of poetic rush. Nothing could surpass the vividness of implied statement about Olive Chancellor's feelings toward Verena Tarrant in *The Bostonians*, a vividness conveyed by the summarizing touch: 'and the vague snow looked cruel'. No more need be said of the relevant sterility and unrealized Lesbian impulse. But too often in James's abundant dramatizations of sexuality the excluded concreteness, the immediacies omitted, lead a subterranean life and proliferate in habits of allegory both too oblique and too obtrusive. What presses on James is an alternative convention, the possibility of graphic statement. George Eliot writes as if *Madame Bovary* had not posed the challenge, had not articulated the poetics of a new relationship between language and the sexual imagination. Henry James cannot afford such indifference. The potentiality of Flaubert weighs on him; he rejects it at the price of intricate, self-conscious labour.

Three *causes célèbres* mark the development of the 'new eroticism' in modern literature: the trial of *Madame Bovary* in January 1857, the decision of the United States District Court in the matter of *Ulysses* in 1933, and the unsuccessful prosecution of *Lady Chatterley's Lover* in London in 1962. From the point of view of literary thought, of the argument between public norms and total imaginative possibility, only Judge Woolsey's ruling on *Ulysses* matters. But the dynamism of total explicitness, the attempt in serious literature to achieve a complete verbal re-presentation of sexuality begins with — or, more accurately, can be defined in respect of — Flaubert (and the indictment, shortly after, of Baudelaire's *Les Fleurs du mal*). The confrontation between public censorship and the claims of the responsible erotic imagination was itself the result of specific and by no means self-evident sociological circumstances. The libertine fiction of the eighteenth century had gone well beyond anything we find in Flaubert; a number of Balzac's novels, such as *Le père Goriot* and *La rabouilleuse*, had silhouetted if not directly rendered motifs of sexual pathology, of scabrous sexual malaise far more lurid than anything in *Madame Bovary*. It was not literature that had changed or swerved to sudden license; the alteration lay in the consolidation of middle-class taste, in the assumption, so characteristic of the mid-nineteenth century, that bourgeois criteria of allowed sensibility, that the emotional habits and norms of mercantile culture, embodied a controlling ideal. With the spread of cheap printing, moreover, and the new breadth of responding literacy, fiction had come to matter. The erotica of the *ancien régime* was élitist, as was the stylized diction in which it was couched. The art of Flaubert was, potentially at least, open to a much wider audience. Hence the subversive vitality of its challenge to the official community of good taste.

It is, at a distance, difficult to recapture outrage. The prosecution conceded Monsieur Flaubert's eminent talent; it was precisely this talent which made his novel so corrupting. 'A moral conclusion cannot make up for lascivious details.' The corset straps whistling snake-like around Emma Bovary's hips, the suave shudder of abandonment with which the young woman surrenders to Rodolphe — these were images that did not discredit realism but the art of fiction itself. 'To impose on art the single rule of public decency is not to make art subservient — it is to do it honour.' Maître Senard's defence of his client bore entirely on the question of motive. *Madame Bovary* is a profoundly moral work. 'Death is in these pages.' Each moment of erotic ecstasy is paid for a hundred-fold in suicidal disgust. The court agreed; whatever the 'reprehensible vulgarity' of local touches, the novel as a whole aimed at a serious, indeed tragic, indictment of adultery. Looking back, Henry James reflected, 'so far have we travelled since then — that *Madame Bovary* should in so comparatively recent a past have been to that extent a cause of reprobation; and suggestive above all, in such connections, as the large unconsciousness of superior minds.' Unconsciousness, no doubt, to the shallow moralism and officious spleen that would greet the book; but not, one supposes, to the radical issues involved.

Flaubert does no less than assert — an assertion the more trenchant for being wholly a matter of mountainous technical labour, of professional *métier* carried to the verge of personal breakdown — that artistic excellence, the high seriousness of the true artist, carries its own complete moral justification. Even as it comes to active being in a sphere strangely between truth and falsehood, the work of art lies outside any code of current ethical convention. It acts on that code, qualifying and re-shaping it towards a more catholic response to human diversity. But it lies outside, and its true morality is internal. The justification of a work of literature is, in the deep sense, technical; it resides in the wealth, difficulty, evocative force of the medium. Trashy prose, be it humanely purposive and moral in the utmost, merits censorship; because its executive means are inferior, because the way in which the thing is done diminishes the reach of the reader's sensibility, because it substitutes the lie of simplification for the exigent intricacy of human fact. Serious fiction and serious poetry cannot be immoral whatever their force of sexual suggestion or savagery of communicated image. Seriousness — a quality demonstrable solely in terms of the fabric itself, of the resources of metaphor drawn upon, of the arduousness and originality of linguistic statement achieved — is the guarantor of relevant morality. Seriously expressed, no 'content' can deprave a mind serious in response. Whatever enriches the adult imagination, whatever complicates consciousness and thus corrodes the *clichés* of daily reflex, is a high moral act. Art is privileged, indeed obliged, to perform this act; it is the live current which splinters and regroups the frozen units of conventional feeling. That — not some modish pose of abdication, of other-worldliness — is the core of *l'art pour l'art*. This morality of enacted form' is the centre and justification of *Madame Bovary*.

Is this assertion of necessary and sufficient internal morality true? Or, rather, what kind of truth does it argue? This, precisely, is the question which besets us a century after *Madame Bovary*, in a context more perplexing and urgent than any envisaged by Flaubert or his accusers. I will come back to it. What needs clarification here is the theory of language, of the relationships between language and imagination operative in the account of sexual experience in Flaubert's novel.

Recognition of the genius of the work has been accompanied, almost from the start, by a measure of discomfort. James found Emma Bovary 'really too small an affair',[1] a vessel too restricted for the subtle profusion of consciousness posited by the novelist. Taking as starting-point Flaubert's own record of his frenetic quest for *le mot juste*, the sentences recast twenty times in an agonized pursuit of uniquely appropriate cadence, Georg Lukács saw in *Madame Bovary* a crisis of confidence, a retreat from that imaginative ease in the real world which distinguishes classic art. Only a sensibility unhoused (which eviction Lukács ascribes to the philistine pressures on the artist of mature capitalism) could invest so passionately, and ultimately despairingly, in the autonomous reality of the word. Sartre's image of Flaubert as literally suffocated in the coils of a perfect style is merely a variant of Lukács's case. Flaubert's chronicle of martyrdom, of the insane pitch of effort at which he laboured to achieve a unique, unflawed authenticity of expressive form, contributes powerfully to the impression of coldness, of still air, many

---

[1] Henry James, 'Gustave Flaubert', in *The Art of Fiction and Other Essays* (Oxford, 1948).

have experienced in reading and re-reading *Madame Bovary*. The death which Flaubert's advocate found in these pages is not merely one of moralizing verdict.

How does Flaubert's ideal of exhaustive explicitness actually work out in regard to the presentment of sexual experience? Going back to the major instances, one realizes by how wide a margin of selective musicality and atmospheric inference Flaubert's narrative departs from any naive *verismo*.

> Çà et là, tout autour d'elle, dans les feuilles ou par terre, des taches lumineuses tremblaient, comme si des colibris, en volant, eussent éparpillé leurs plumes. Le silence était partout, quelque chose de doux semblait sortir des arbres; elle sentait son cœur, dont les battements recommenceaient, et le sang circuler dans sa chair comme un fleuve de lait. Alors, elle entendit tout au loin, au delà du bois, sur les autres collines, un cri vague et prolongé, une voix qui se trainait, et elle l'écoutait silencieusement, se mêlant comme une musique aux dernières vibrations de ses nerfs émus. Rodolphe, le cigare aux dents, raccommodait avec son canif une des deux brides cassée.[1]

> (Here and there around her the leaves were dappled with a flickering brightness as though humming-birds had shed their wings in flight. Silence was everywhere. Sweetness seemed to breathe from the trees. She felt her heart beginning to beat again, and the blood flowing inside her flesh like a river of milk. Then far away beyond the forest, on the other side of the valley, she heard a strange, long-drawn cry that hung on the air, and she listened to it in silence as it mingled like music with the last vibrations of her jangled nerves. Rodolphe, cigar in mouth, was mending one of the bridles with his pocket-knife.)

The Freudian valuations of that 'river of milk' or of that cigar between the lover's teeth are undeniable, as are the allegoric, traditional counters such as the broken bridle. But the specific miracle of the passage lies in Flaubert's simulation of Emma's return to consciousness after the sexual act. It is a simulation achieved by means of rhythm and image. The modulations in the past tenses of the verbs, the utterly deliberate punctua-

---

[1] Gustave Flaubert, *Madame Bovary* (Paris, 1857), Pt. II, Ch. ix.

tion and adjustment in the lengths of successive clauses, enforce on our own breathing, on the imitative somatic stance by which a reader responds to a suggested series of images, an exact counterpart to Emma Bovary's ebbing sensuality and tranquil, yet delicately haunted, peace. The symbolic properties invoked precisely sustain the intended feeling: that lengthy, vague cry beyond the woods resounds at moments lyric and ominous throughout Romantic literature. We hear a last ironic echo of it in the twang of the broken string in *The Cherry Orchard*. The humming-bird plumage and dim softness out of the trees in the smouldering sunset (*dans la rougeur du soir*) belong to the stylized ecstasies of Romantic verse and fiction. Flaubert's use of them is adroit; they reflect both outward to our own sensibility and inward to the rhetoric of romance on which Emma Bovary feeds — a rhetoric precisely located for us by the fact that Emma, on returning home, immediately falls to dreaming of 'the lyric legion' of adulterous heroines. In short, the reality of the passage is sensuously overwhelming. It elicits from us emotions, a physical and psychological *mimesis*, exactly correspondent to the narrative. But the reality is not one of obvious verbal facsimile. The rhythms are vividly, directly suggestive (as they are again in the notorious carriage-ride with Léon), not the actual terms used. Flaubert's eroticism is a matter of cadence. It is the theory of total expression, therefore, rather than the actual practice of *Madame Bovary* which proved exemplary.

In Flaubert, as in Baudelaire, the pursuit of explicitness was not an end in itself but part of a rigorous morality of aesthetic form. The explicitness achieved was still governed by considerations of stylistic elegance. In Maupassant, Zola, and the naturalistic movement, explicitness of a new, far more literal order breaks through. Integrity of representation came to replace integrity of artistic form as the essential criterion of seriousness. To say less than all was to abdicate from the novelist's intellectual and social function. The naturalistic writer saw himself as the peer of the physical scientist and analytic historian; his novels had to communicate a correspondingly anatomical and unflinching view of human affairs. No less than Symbolism (though the two movements are exactly opposed in their aesthetics) Naturalism moved on a wave of conscious anti-philistinism. To shock the bourgeois, to challenge the taboos of respectable speech, became an obligation. For his part the enlightened reader – 'mon semblable, – mon frère!' – demonstrated his maturity and toughness of sensibility by concealing his shock or, indeed, spurring the artist to new audacities. The passage from *le mot juste* to *le mot exact* in the 1870s and 1880s was the result of a mutually accelerating impulse of both writer and reader. To that impulse increasingly graphic means of reproduction and direct reportage – the modern newspaper story, the photograph – brought a competitive challenge. To keep its grip on a public stimulated by but soon almost immune to all but the grossest intensities of journalistic description, the novel had to pass from image to picture. Hence the photographic insistence of the Goncourts, of Maupassant, and of Zola. A drastic advance toward erotic verisimilitude separates the language of *Nana* from that of Flaubert:

Nana se pelotonnait sur elle-même. Un frisson de tendresse semblait avoir passé dans ses membres. Les yeux mouillés, elle se faisait petite, comme pour se mieux sentir. Puis, elle dénoua les mains, les abaissa le long d'elle par un glissement, jusqu'aux seins, qu'elle écrasa d'une étreinte nerveuse. Et rengorgée, se fondant dans une caresse de tout son corps, elle se frotta les joues à droite, à gauche, contre ses épaules, avec câlinerie. Sa bouche goulue soufflait sur elle le désir. Elle allongea les lèvres, elle se baisa longuement près de l'aisselle. . . . Alors, Muffat eut un soupir bas et prolongé. . . . Il prit Nana à bras le corps, dans un élan de brutalité, et la jeta sur le tapis.[1]

[1] Emile Zola, *Nana* (Paris, 1880), Ch. VII.

(Nana gathered herself into a ball. A shiver of tenderness seemed to have passed through her limbs. Moist-eyed, she made herself small so as to feel her body more closely. Then she unclasped her hands and slid them down her body as far as her breasts, which she crushed in a nervous embrace. Her breasts out-thrust and as if melting into a caress of her entire body, Nana cuddled her cheeks, first right then left, against her shoulders. Her greedy mouth breathed desire across her own flesh. She pointed her lips and kissed herself, unhurriedly, near her armpits. . . . Muffat breathed a low, prolonged sigh. . . . He seized Nana, in a brutal rush, and threw her onto the carpet.)

Flaubert saw in *Nana* the triumphant culmination of an idéal of sexual candour which he himself had initiated and enforced on a hypocritical society: 'que la table d'hôte des tribades "révolte toute pudeur," je le crois! Et bien! Après! merde pour les imbéciles.'

Changes in the middle-class tolerance of sexual shock, the reluctance of the *imbéciles* to reveal themselves as such, whatever their private feelings, were hastened by an almost automatic linguistic mechanism. From *Nana* to *Ulysses* and *Lady Chatterley's Lover*, from *Lady Chatterley* to *Last Exit to Brooklyn*, a constant progression toward the limits of sexual explicitness is at work. Each advance brings with it, by a compulsive logic of formal structure, the need to take the next step, to bring verbal means another bit closer to complete erotic re-enactment (even as each increase of nakedness and allowed posture in the cinema or photography has brought us nearer to the open representation of intercourse). Flaubert and his naturalistic successors had set off a self-perpetuating dynamic inside the idiom of the novel. Often writer and audience exaggerate the spontaneity, the deliberate moral courage of the latest frankness. In the whole process a powerful linguistic automatism is manifest.

Since about 1890 homosexuality has played a vital part in Western culture and, perhaps even more significantly, in the myths and emblematic gestures which that culture has used in order to arrive at self-consciousness. Artists who have covertly or publicly practised pæderasty and/or various modes of adult homo-eroticism hold an important, at certain points predominant place in modern literature, art, music, ballet, and in the minor or decorative arts. The tonality of the 'modern movement', the theories of the creative act implicit in important branches of twentieth-century arts and letters, cannot be dissociated from the lives and work of Oscar Wilde, Proust, André Gide, Stefan George, and Cocteau. From early rhapsodies or masques of Gide to the poetry of Allen Ginsberg and the fiction of James Purdy, James Baldwin, and William Burroughs, explicit homosexuality or homosexuality symbolically declared, activates much that is most distinctive of the sensibility of the age. Why?

The phenomenon itself has been extensively studied; its causes and central energies remain obscure. It can be argued that the problem is one of optics, that homosexuality played no less of a role in Periclean Athens or Renaissance Florence, that the cultural élite of the rococo was no less inclined to homosexuality than the world of Diaghilev: the difference being, simply, one of the data available. But although there is something in this and although the salience of modern homosexuality is in part a visual effect — the surrounding medium of middle-class norms and a simultaneous loosening of verbal and legal taboos have made homosexuality more prominent — the facts are more stubborn and intricate. From *art nouveau* to 'camp' and Gay Lib, homosexual codes and ideals are a major force. They seem to underlie, as if re-enacting their own solipsism, their own physiological and social enclosedness, that most characteristic of modern strategies: the poem whose real subject is the poem, art that is about self-possibility, ornament and architecture that have as their main referent not some grid of actual human use but other ornament or other form. So far as much of the best, of the most original in modern art and literature is autistic, i.e. unable or unwilling to look to a reality or 'normality' outside its own chosen rules, so far as much of the modern genius can be understood from the point of view of a sufficiently comprehensive, sophisticated theory of games, there is in it a radical homosexuality. In other words, homosexuality could be construed as a creative rejection of the philosophic and conventional realism, of the *mundanity* and extroversion of classic and nineteenth-century feeling. That feeling produces works of art and literature which 'look outward' for their meaning and validity, which accept authorities and solicit approvals outside themselves. The painting aims to 'look like something in the real world,' the poem has a final basis of verification in prose paraphrase or common sense, music has structures powerfully analogous to the syntax of common discourse. Heterosexuality is the very essence of such classic realism, of art and language that are centrally acts of communication, of relationship to the 'outside'. Where poetics after Mallarmé turn inward, where the subject of a painting becomes painting, where music and dance reject translation into any alphabet of exterior meaning, they seem to express needs and conceptions of self-sufficient form deeply related to homosexuality or to that abstraction of homosexuality which is narcissism. The mirrors of the modern shine inward in a probing, tormenting meditation on the self or on that 'other' like enough to be its shadow (in Proust and Cocteau the iconography of 'enclosedness' and the rules of the mirror-game are most consciously worked out).

On a simpler level, the homosexual current in post-symbolist literature may be understood as a strategy of opposition, as the artist's most emphatic stance against philistinism. Such a stance, which the artist himself often finds indispensable to sustain his creative solitude, became increasingly difficult to adopt as puritanism weakened. In the Romantic period the mere choice of art or literature as a mode of life had been enough to assert a rebellious eccentricity, a dissent from the social norm. Flaubert already found the process of necessary dissociation more difficult and made a constant, if muted, rebellion of the obsessive mania of his work. In Poe and Baudelaire drugs provide a haven, which is also an exile, outside the frontiers of the bourgeois order. As the artist became accepted, his rebellions blunted by the indifference or conventionalized shock of the now sophisticated public, his task of self-definition grew more arduous. Where could he find a genuine extra-territoriality, a posture genuinely offensive (in the sense both of attack and of provoked outrage)? The Verlaine-Rimbaud scandal and the career of Oscar Wilde gave to homosexuality representative, strategic values. The homosexual overlapped with the artist in being an outsider, a 'grand refuser' of those standards of creativity and utilitarian relationship which define middle-class, industrial, post-Puritan civilization. Homosexuality in part made possible that exercise in solipsism, that remorseless mockery of philistine common sense and bourgeois realism which is modern art. As the twentieth century progresses other externalities, other 'offending/offensive exiles' such as those of the Jew and of the Negro come to serve as strategic functions for the writer and artist. A common narcissism and subversion relates these different creative masks. But whatever its sources, the homosexual current has produced much, one is tempted to say a major part, of what will stand in the treatment of love in modern literature.

Looking back at *Death in Venice* from the vantagepoint of present overtness, one is struck by the hushed ceremony of the story, by Thomas Mann's unworried exploitation of allegoric pointers — the Wagnerian reference of the title, Aschenbach's name, the death-ship, the orgiastic nightmare, naked *amor* risen from the sea — no longer available to our 'knowingness' (it is in the passage from knowledge to 'knowingness' that I am trying to locate our theme). The tale looks back to civilizing encumbrances and dreams of reason which Mann knew to be doomed. Nevertheless it would be myopic to underestimate its sexual audacity. In a manner comparable to the love poetry of Donne, *Death in Venice* articulates, perhaps rediscovers, a death-haunted eroticism, a *morbidezza* in which a crisis of desire is made expressive of a far wider disorder of human values. The master of style discovers the intrusive inadequacy of speech: 'Aschenbach understood not a word he said; it might be the sheerest commonplace, in his hearing it became mingled harmonies.' The naked radiance of the boy liberates the great writer from 'the marble mass of language'. Eros overwhelms him: 'Mind and heart were drunk with passion, his footsteps guided by the daemonic power whose pastime it is to trample on human reason and dignity.' The betraying egoism of Aschenbach's experience, the fact that it is on Tadzio's mere shadow that he lavishes 'lover-like, endearing terms' — there is never between the old man and the boy either touch or speech — only reinforces the mortal intensity of lust. Though explicitly linked to the poetic, partially allegoric paedophilia of the Platonic dialogues and the Socratic myth of *eros*, Mann's novella seems to initiate a series of similar narratives. From Gide's *Les faux-monnayeurs* to Nabokov's *Lolita* modern fiction has produced a number of remarkable realizations of an adult's sexual relation to a child or group of children. These encounters are almost invariably homo-erotic and it may be Nabokov's reversal that gives to *Lolita* some of its unsettling sparkle.

The case of Marcel Proust can hardly be touched on in a brief survey. But it is striking how largely Proust studies, voluminous and often intelligent as they are, have failed to grasp the nettle. The affair between the narrator and Albertine is one — and there are obviously not many in the history of art and literature — that literally enlarges the resources of our sensibility, that actually educates our recognitions to new possibilities of feeling. Proust has widened the repertoire of sexual consciousness. Areas of adolescent sexuality, of imaginary possession, of jealousy, of sexual loss have, through Proust's formulation, become larger or newly accessible. As is the uncanny case with very great art, *A la recherche du temps perdu* has acted as a prescriptive mythology, calling into being nuances of emotion, twists of being and pretence, which were, somehow, a *terra incognita* of the self. Biographical information, in the matter of Proust over-abundant and therefore obscuring, leads one to suppose that Albert lives formidably in Albertine. The young woman, feminine and rounded as she is, masks what is, in some sense, the subterranean, more direct truth of homosexual love. So André Gide felt in his strictures on Proust's 'insincerity'. But the facts are even more tangled. We know that Albertine does incorporate the traits of women whom Proust knew and who, at some level of perceptual enchantment, meant much to him. Thus the foremost celebration of love in twentieth century literature is ambiguous to the core. But not ambiguous in any shallow, tactical sense manipulated by a critic. The Albert-Albertine figure, the narrator's transpositions between heterosexual and homosexual codes, belong to that strange suspension of sexual difference or rather to that fusion of erotic being which we find at certain particular summits in the Western tradition. The mysterious completeness of Proust's eroticism, mysterious because it is also an artifice, relates to the myth of sexual unison in the *Symposium*, to the androgynous conceit in some of Leonardo da Vinci's representations of the human figure, to the interchangeability and co-presence of masculine and feminine in some of the poetry and drama of Marlowe, of Shakespeare, and of Goethe's amorous elegies. Where our imagination moves deepest it strives beyond sexuality, which is, inevitably, division, to an erotic whole.

It is precisely against this wholeness, not against any simple heterosexuality, that Proust sets off the torturing incompletion of Sodom and Gomorrah. His detailed mapping of homosexual and Lesbian life and society has within it a moralizing, damning force. Charlus has an immensity of presence denied to Vautrin not only because Proust can go further than Balzac — he can detail the world of perversion in a way unavailable to the idiom of the 1830s — but because he is making a persistent tragic statement about the nature of human love itself. Because he is setting out, as Plato and Shakespeare did, the dialectic of identity and desire: how may we reach the beloved without destroying something of that principle of self from which love springs? In the homosexual and the Lesbian that paradox is frozen to sterile acceptance. The broken sphere of Plato's myth is made a treadmill. One need only re-read the close of the first chapter of *Sodome et Gomorrhe* to experience the underlying grimness of Proust's vision of Sodom and why total (therefore unattainable) communication with, total (therefore unattainable) possession of the beloved, becomes to the narrator the very meaning of life. Thus Proust's homosexuality, though vitally significant, animates, as Gide's or Cocteau's does not, imagined, a poetically experienced, completeness of love.

In Jean Genet there is no such completeness. On the contrary, there is a fierce striving for partiality, for the special point of view. The homosexual, criminal underground of Genet's novels defines itself by its derisive 'otherness' (*altérité*). Its relation to established society is one of subversive travesty. Hence the dominant function of disguise, charades, masks, and transvestism in Genet's art. Above all,

this travesty inspires Genet's talent for high rhetoric, his use
of the French language at its most formal, of French prosody
where it is most like Victor Hugo, to brazen the unspeakable.
Genet makes every brutality and obscenity of homosexual
relations explicit, but in a special highly original way. By
spelling out *everything* in a style of lyric declamation, he
creates a kind of solid, graphic unreality — as does a painting
by Caravaggio. In Genet homosexuality becomes a 'garden of
love', divorced from ordinary society less by its bestial
violence and elaborate slang than by its intense stylization,
by the terrain it affords for play-acting, festive ceremonies,
and unbridled pathos. Genet is heir to Maeterlinck and Yeats,
to those who have sought a stage for action more formal,
more rigorously aesthetic than that provided by realism.
Reticence is one kind of stylization; total explicitness is
another:

> Élève-toi dans l'air de la lune, o ma gosse.
> Viens couler dans ma bouche un peu de sperme lourd
> Qui roule de ta gorge à mes dents, mon Amour,
> Pour féconder enfin nos adorables noces.
>
> Colle ton corps ravi contre le mien qui meurt
> D'enculer la plus tendre et douce des fripouilles.
> En soupesant charmé tes rondes, blondes couilles,
> Mon vit de marbre noir t'enfile jusqu' au cœur.
>
> (Rise in the moonlight, my sweek jocko. Come and
> let a little heavy semen drip into my mouth, rolling
> from your throat to my teeth, Beloved, so as to make
> fruitful at last our adorable wedding. Glue your
> ravishing body against my dying flesh, dying to
> bugger the most tender and sweet of rogues. While
> charmed I weigh your round, blond balls, my black
> marble prick shafts you to the heart.)

It is impossible to 'go further' than does *Le condamné à mort*.
Yet such is the elevation of tone — with its echoes, at once

parodistic and scholastic, of Victor Hugo, Rimbaud, and even Péguy — that the category of obscenity does not seem to fit. It is where the brazen singularity of vision falters, where naturalism and mere reportage corrupt style, that the matter of obscenity or motive arises (as it does in John Rechy's *City of Night* and Hubert Selby's *Last Exit to Brooklyn*, two books very probably inspired by Genet). Genet has made of violent, totally promiscuous buggery a world, a dramatic form, fantastic yet relevant by virtue or ironic mime to the mendacities and savageries of our normal, respectable condition.

Homosexuality has not been the only indirection of love explored by modern literature. The rapid erosion of verbal and representational taboos that follows on the work of Havelock Ellis, Krafft-Ebing, and Freud has brought types of erotic behaviour previously restricted to straight pornography, to the twilit zone of *curiosa* and popular ethnography, or to forensic medicine into the repertoire of serious literature. It is difficult to think of any mode of sexual action — bestial, fetishistic, sadomasochistic, incestuous — that has not been shown in modern fiction or drama. Incest is, in the Freudian reading, a primary structure in evolving human consciousness. It has a dim but unmistakable centrality in Greek tragic mythology. In the return to Greek motifs of modern drama, incest has figured prominently. The richest, most humanely serious treatment of a brother-sister passion may be seen in Robert Musil's novel *Der Mann ohne Eigenschaften*. The work is incomplete and we cannot be certain that Ulrich and Agathe would have consummated their tense, searching need of each other. But what fragments we have of a third volume, especially the broken, dance-like exchange by moonlight, suggest Musil's broad grasp of the theme, his aim to make of it, as often in contemporary literature, a symbol of love seeking total communion, total privacy from the 'otherness'

124 On Difficulty and Other Essays

of the world. A comparable equivalence between brother-sister incest and the general drama of human isolation can be seen, though on a slighter scale, in Cocteau's *Les enfants terribles* and Sartre's *Les séquestrés d'Altona*.

Clearly, however, it is in its uses of cruelty, of the sadistic components or aberrations of sexuality, that modern literature has gone furthest. Sadistic motifs and their interweaving with the erotic are perennial in art and literature; they play a pronounced role in the baroque and Gothic sensibilities. The image of love as a torturer, of a secret analogy between lover and beloved and torturer and tortured, seems archetypal to human consciousness. We find it memorably enacted in Hieronymus Bosch's gardens of delight. But the modern focus is different, at once more diffuse and more specific in its concentration on sadism in sexual phantasy and private life. From, say, Zola's *L'assommoir* (1878) to Pauline Réage's *L'histoire d'O* (1954) and William Burroughs's *The Naked Lunch* (1959), the explicitness of sadistic action has increased continually. Phantasies and presumed realities which had been the stock-in-trade of pornography have passed intact into serious literature. Sade has become both a dramatic emblem of man 'at the outer edge' and the object of a modish philosophic and literary cult. I have written elsewhere[1] of some aspects of this obsessive imaginative exploitation of cruelty and erotic humiliation. Only the main points can be referred to here. Few topics provoke a more confident display of liberal cant. We simply *do not know* whether or to what degree sadistic literature initiates or quickens imitative behaviour (work under way on this question in clinical psychology is, as yet, rudimentary but results suggest that there *may* be a relationship between sadistic suggestion and subsequent conduct). The claim that sadistic literature merely induces masturbation and thus diminishes the

[1] G.Steiner, *Language and Silence* (London and New York, 1970).

individual or social potential for sadistic action may or may not be valid. It cannot, in either case, be naively generalized. The impact of sadistic proposals on the literate, otherwise engaged or furnished sensibility is wholly different from such impact on those whose imaginative lives are barren, hollowed by monotony, or ill-equipped to handle the conventions of unreality in a printed text (here the evidence of the Moors murder case seems pertinent).

The literary historian asks a different question: is the theme of cruelty and the associated obsession with violence in some way related to the political character of the age? Genet, Norman Mailer, William Burroughs have said that the bestialities recounted in their work mirror the crisis of inhumanity through which we appear to be living since 1914. A literature which failed to reflect modern barbarism, the widespread return of torture in political life, the programmatic degradation of the human person in concentration camps and colonial wars, would be a lie. There is unquestionably a truth in this argument. But it is not easy to judge whether the literature of violence does not at times anticipate, almost conjure up the facts (Céline would be a case in point), and whether anything is gained by adding, even in phantasy, to the energies of the inhuman.

Where the modern imagination *has* gone deeper than that of any previous age (though the recognition itself is as old as Aeschylus) is in its depiction of love and sexual encounter as power relations. We know more plainly than before, because Strindberg, Proust, D.H.Lawrence, and Beckett have taught us, that sexual relations are, in the sphere of intimacy, a reproduction of conflicts, alliances, strategic manœuvres as we find them in social and economic relations. The symbolic, psychosomatic links between sexuality and money are foreshadowed in Ben Jonson and explicit in Swift. But the close cross-hatching of social or economic metaphors with the 'spontaneities' of love is very much a part of the development of the modern novel. We locate it first in Balzac and George Eliot; it is superbly exploited in James's *The Wings of the Dove* and *The Golden Bowl*. Where erotic codes become more problematic, where power relations and the struggle for sexual domination sharpen, the sadistic motif — at its serious, tragic level — arises. Nowhere is the theme of erotic torment, this 'daily pathology' of love, more powerfully dramatized, more illuminatingly related to economic and class conflicts than in John Cowper Powys's *A Glastonbury Romance*. The *Romance* and *Wolf Solent* mark perhaps the only 'advance', if such a term can be used, of the sexual imagination beyond Dostoevsky and Proust. The eroticism of Powys is at once more extreme and more delicate than anything we find in Lawrence, but it is obscured by a private, often portentous rhetoric. If it were better known, 'The River' chapter in the *Romance*, with its display of a 'cold-blooded and elemental lechery', would have focussed many of the wonders and outrages lavished on the naiveties of *Lady Chatterley's Lover*. Like the famous suppressed chapter of *The Possessed*, 'The Iron Bar' in the *Romance* seeks out the dark common root of the nerve of cruelty and the nerve of desire. Owen Evans, like Powys himself, is half-crazed with sadistic imaginings. Cordelia Geard announces that she is with child:

'What shall we call him if he's a boy, Owen?' Her voice just then was more than he could bear. Nothing makes human nerves dance with such blind fury as a voice piercing the hollow of the ear at the moment when the will is stretched out like a piece of India rubber on the rack of indecision.

'Torture!' he shouted, sitting up in the purple chair and clutching its elbows furiously, while the rim of her hat was now completely crushed beneath him. 'We'll call him Torture; and if she's a girl we'll call her Finis, the End. For she'll *be* the end. And all is the end.'

There ensues one of the strangest, most compelling scenes of

love-making in modern fiction. Ungainly, bewildered, yet
instinctively clairvoyant, Cordy pulls off her clothes. She
stirs 'some deep chord of excited desire in the man with the
bruning eyes'. Sexuality triumphs over sadism by enclosing it,
by touching a common root, deep as life, inextricable as are
within us the need to possess and the need to destroy.

It is not, however, in the treatment of deviance or sexual
pathology that common sense would locate the most obvious, prodigal element of the new literary freedom. It
is in the explicit rendition, particularly in the novel, of
heterosexual intercourse. In a hundred years we have
moved from the suggestive paraphrase of *Madame Bovary* —
suggestive mainly in its hints of imitative cadence and in
its invocation of symbolic props — to the following (two
passages representative, current enough to have been chosen
almost at random):

It turned into a very serious session, no memorable jokes or clever ideas.
He just stayed on top of her, embracing her buttocks to get her pressed
against him and opening her cunt with his broad stiff staff. He got the
head of his cock into the centre of her sex, and stayed on it, rubbed on
it, without mercy. . . . Her spread legs pulled together and locked him
to her, and her perspiring body got ready for the second time. . . . He
fucked her until she was a hot river, until he could feel her not knowing
or caring who or what the thing inside of her was. . . .[1]

. . . I turned her over suddenly on her belly, my avenger wild . . . holding
her prone against the mattress with the strength of my weight, I drove
into the seat of all stubbornness, tight as a vice, and I wounded her, I
knew it, she thrashed beneath me like a trapped little animal, making
not a sound, but fierce not to allow me this last of the liberties, and yet
caught, forced to give up millimetre by millimetre the bridal ground of
her symbolic and therefore real vagina. So I made it, I made it all the
way—it took ten minutes and maybe more, but as the avenger rode
down to his hilt . . . she gave a last little cry of farewell, and I could feel

[1] Harriet Daimter (pseud.), 'The Woman Thing', in *The Olympia Reader* (New
York, 1965).

a new shudder which began as a ripple, and rolled into a wave, and then it rolled over her. . . .[1]

The chronology of the change, of the successive advances towards total explicitness, is complex and would repay detailed study. The work of Zola and Maupassant marked a deliberate expansion of sexual designation. In so far as it addressed itself to the physicality of man, to society as biologically determined, the entire naturalistic movement — Gorky, Dreiser, Hauptmann — tended to a new erotic frankness. When the 'breakthrough' comes, in *Ulysses,* in *Lady Chatterley's Lover,* in the writings of Céline and Henry Miller, it does so on an explicitly linguistic level. The turn of sensibility toward a complete probing of sexual experience, the conviction that such experience is inseparable from the felt life of fiction, are manifest in Flaubert. The steps taken by Joyce or D.H.Lawrence are 'technical', though in a sense that involves an entire philosophy of language and literary form. The taboos challenged and exorcised are those of vocabulary. What passes in the 'place of excrement' and love itself are seen to be four-letter words, and are spelt out. What follows on Molly Bloom's reveries and the bucolics of Lady Chatterley is strictly inevitable, a *passage à la limite* in an almost algebraic sense. Given the new dispensation, each generation of fiction has gone a step further toward totality, toward *saying all* in words as graphic, as exact as the language can provide. There are stages on this *via amorosa.* William Faulkner's *Sanctuary* (1931) and realistic crime fiction, related as they are to film and pulp writing, introduce a new authenticity of erotic slang and a cold, precise bawdy. The American novel comes out of World War II charged with a graphic economy of speech. By the late 1950s the semantic battles fought by

[1] Norman Mailer, 'The Time of Her Time', in *Advertisements for Myself* (New York and London, 1959).

Joyce and Lawrence had been won. No word, no turn of phrase was inviolate or exempt from public use. In Doris Lessing's *The Golden Notebook*, one of the finest novels written in English since the war, Ella is shown in a mood not wholly unlike Jane Austen's Emma:

Now she cannot sleep, she masturbates, to accompaniment of fantasies of hatred about men. Paul has vanished completely: she has lost the warm strong man of her experience, and can only remember a cynical betrayer. She suffers sex desire in a vacuum. She is acutely humiliated, thinking that this means she is dependent on men for 'having sex', for 'being serviced', for 'being satisfied'. She uses this kind of savage phrase to humiliate herself.[1]

The delicate comedy of the passage, a comedy distinctly akin to *Emma*, lies precisely in the fact that these phrases are not 'savage', that they echo a lost gentility, or rather a phase of mere 'adult frankness' before total explicitness.

The sociological and psychological correlatives of this 'frankness as never before' lie outside the scope of this essay. They are very large. What failures of nerve in humane literacy, what distrust of the imagination, has brought on this obsessive, philosophically naïve investment in the word? How does the common use, and hence devaluation, of what were, for a long time, the 'private parts' of speech, the taboo idiom of intimacy or subterranean argot, relate to the much larger political, commercial, scientific assaults on privacy that mark our century? Or is there, on the contrary, an endeavour to strip such words of their numinous force, to bring language to daylight as Freud had brought the symbolic vocabularies of the unconscious? And in what way would such 'enlightenment' relate to mass democracy, to a society intent on levelling taste? For the sense of audacity registered by the writer — when and especially when he insists on breaking a previous

[1] Doris Lessing, *The Golden Notebook* (London, 1962).

verbal taboo — is not one felt by the less educated, less priviledged classes. To them the discourse of love has long been monosyllabic. To what extent is the accelerated movement toward complete explicitness in literature only a logical consequence of a movement of all narrative forms toward the techniques of the cinema? In other words, is sexual frankness in prose fiction merely another attempt at 'verbal photography', at competing in language with the total *verismo* available to the camera and the tape-recorder? (In which context it is worth noting how closely the sexual revelations of such documentary records as Professor Oscar Lewis's *La Vida* now seem to resemble those imagined by novelists. The tape starts imitating the *cliché* of fiction.) What bearing has all this on the life of the imagination, a concept which has, I believe, a politically relevant and verifiable meaning? Already there is some evidence, though difficult to assess, of a standardization in sexual behaviour, of a decline from individuality and private discovery in this most inward, most vulnerable of psychic resources. Banality and brutality of idiom diminish the reach, the wondrous specificity of individual human consciousness. At the same time the new mythology of orgasm, of sexual prowess and ardent receptivity, may be setting standards of expectation, routines of high hope, in fact realizable by no more than a minority of human beings. So far as most ordinary men and women are concerned, the largesse and publicized splendours of the new sexuality are a lie, perhaps as corrosive as were the repressive daemonologies of puritanism or the cant (often exaggerated) of the Victorians.

The literary historian deals with smaller questions, though anyone seriously engaging problems of language touches on the human fact in its widest implications. How may one assess the effect of the new total freedom on the state of literary form, particularly of the novel?

In the art of Jane Austen a stylized idiom — stylized most coherently by what it excluded — served as a contract of permissible expectation between novelist and reader. The stability of vision which such a contract affords enabled the writer to work both economically and exhaustively; the area defined for imaginative penetration could be superbly exploited. But it was a limited terrain, better suited to the framework of stage comedy, with its necessarily public standards of speech, than to the new means and opportunities of the novel. Too much was left unsaid and, therefore, unrealized; or, more precisely, that which was excluded from the available vocabulary entailed additional omissions even wider in scope. Jane Austen's notorious indifference to the fierce historical, social crises which surround her life and her fiction is no accident, no contingent convention. It relates immediately to the exclusion of the new sense, so actively developing in the early nineteenth century, of the erotic and the unconscious. Jane Austen applies the same excluding idiom to the power relations of politics, class, and money as she does to those of sexuality — an idiom no longer consonant with the demands and possibilities of insight as we find them, say, in Stendhal. She keeps at bay, through a specific code of permissible expression, disorders of sensibility — erotic, financial, political — which would have marred the profound discipline and fineness of her design, but made of it a larger thing. The arrow that strikes Emma hits clean and sharp but passes too easily through a medium as thin and unambiguous as are the silhouettes prized by Jane Austen's genteel contemporaries.

The major, the 'classic' phase of the novel, as it extends from George Eliot to Conrad, the early D.H.Lawrence, and Thomas Mann, seems to me inseparable from a definite creative tension between idiom and consciousness in the erotic domain. When we consider *Middlemarch, The Portrait of a Lady, Anna Karenina, Nostromo, The Rainbow, The Magic Mountain*, we are made aware of a distinctive completeness or erotic intelligence. The novelist's view of the human person, of psychic processes, of the centrality of sexual experience, comes through to us at every point. Nothing germane to the psychological, social context need be omitted. The language of the novelist is comprehensive of all requisite perception; we sense immediately 'behind' or within it a formidable, entirely verifiable, gathering of felt knowledge.

'Behind' or within it; this is my point. The explicitness is complete but *internal*. The failure of the Karenin marriage is drastic; the hurt and specificity of sexual crisis presses on the reader. But such are the authority and density of the medium, of the world which Tolstoy builds around each imaginative fact, that the crisis is conveyed to us through the simplest of images — a fire dying in the grate. The threefold relationship of Isabel Archer, Madame Merle, and Gilbert Osmond draws on elements of sadism, of sexual torment, of voyeurism as raw as any in present fiction. We are allowed no escape from the cruel insistence of James's understanding. But again, the relevant statements are made 'internally'; it is the fullness and clear focus of invoked imagery, the control of relevant tone which informs not the use of sexual termonology. The pathology of sex in Mann's novel is exact and pervasive. But the 'facts' about Claudia Chauchat or Mynheer Peeperkorn are communicated to us inside, as it were, the clarity, the strange cruel innocence of myth. No semantic 'photography' is required. Undeniably, this distance between sexual awareness and idiom did pose problems for the novelist. I have suggested that the proliferating symbolism and paraphrases of James point to an unresolved inadequacy of expressive means; a similar malaise may be accountable for the portentous lyricism and obliquity of some of Conrad. But in *Middlemarch*, in *Anna Karenina*, in *The Bostonians*, in *Sons and Lovers*, the tension between the known and the 'out-spoken' produces a shapely stress and poise of imagination. And it is, by necessary extension, a poise and stress which allows, indeed compels the inclusion in the novel of political, economic, social reality. If the classic novel has produced an image of society more adequately complex and informed than any other in literature or history, it is precisely because it extends to society, to life as a whole, the organic view it takes of human love or human hatred. Sexual intelligence, kept so by avoidance of the falsifications of gross, explicit vocabularies, becomes political intelligence in the truest sense — in the sense of Stendhal, George Eliot, Tolstoy and the early Lawrence.

The change to a new verbal freedom, the drive for complete designation, as it leads from *Lady Chatterley's Lover* to Norman Mailer, has brought changes to the metaphysic, if that term is allowed, of the novel — changes first discernible in Flaubert's view of *Madame Bovary*. The contemporary novelist controls his characters as the classic novelist does not. This is a difficult point to make clearly, but its meaning — as Tolstoy has testified when noting the autonomous, scandalous vitality and 'resistance' of his personages — is more than metaphoric. Every writer 'invents' and thus governs the agents of his fiction, but George Eliot, Henry James, and Tolstoy seem to leave around men and women a zone of unexplored freedom, a kind of inviolate spring of independent life. This effect derives, I believe, from a crucial notion of privacy. There are elements, particularly sexual elements, in their personages which the great novelists fully realize but do not verbalize. They seem to accord to their own imaginings a certain privilege of discretion. It is by virtue of a discretion closely similar to that which we show toward other human beings that the fictions of *Middlemarch* or *War and Peace* —

complex, rounded, never wholly known or mastered — stay with us. George Eliot, Henry James, and Tolstoy allow us, demand from us, a serious collaboration, because they signify completely but do not say, let alone shout, all. They draw our sensibility into a collaborative response. We imagine and, in some modest degree, we 'create with them'. We are neither found out nor expertly embarrassed in the act of reading (such embarrassment of the reader being a characteristic tactic of the new eroticism). The novelist guards our freedom of imaginative life as he does that of his characters. In the 'new freedom' there is more than a touch of bullying. Our imaginings are programmed, obscene words are shouted at the inner ear. The new idiom has made it difficult to distinguish between integrity and mendacity. Of two passages quoted earlier (pp. 127–8), which is by a master of contemporary prose, which by a pseudonymous hack? Audacity, four-letter eloquence has rapidly become a *cliché*, a formulaic gesture as predictable as Petrarchan love-rhetoric and less varied. Loudness is poverty. *Doctor Zhivago* is not, at every point, a persuasive novel; we are asked to extend to the hero assumptions of poetic genius and corresponding political insight in fact appropriate only to Pasternak himself. Nevertheless, the relationship of Zhivago and Lara has assumed an almost magical authority in the modern poetics of love. Readers have felt here a maturity, a completeness of sexual realization hardly to be found elsewhere. Yet Pasternak's treatment is reticent in the extreme. His silences, like those of Tolstoy or Mann, seem to create meaning. The violences, the gusts of terror which surround Zhivago and Lara are as radical as any invoked in Mailer's *The American Dream* or in *Last Exit to Brooklyn*. We emerge from both shaken, and, perhaps, instructed. But by calling on us to imagine, to give echo from the experienced if unspoken truths of our own privacies, Pasternak leaves us freer than he found us. A sexual idiom free from compulsive literalness is, I think, vital to this liberating effect.

The present code of sexual explicitness may be related to the general malaise of the novel. The inhumanities of speech and action so obsessively reproduced in many important contemporary novels have, as their natural counterpoint, the 'non-humanity' of the *nouveau roman*. The human person is as splintered, as used and deformed in many modern novels as it is in certain schools of twentieth-century painting and sculpture. It is as absent from the *nouveau roman* (or at least its theories) as from non-representational art. We have added many words to the vocabulary of fiction and drama. We say and show all (or will do so next month, next week). Have we lost the curious wonder of an imagined living presence, the paradox of reality by which Anna Karenina or Isabel Archer outlive their begetters and will outlive us? The 'sexual revolution' in twentieth-century speech, literature, and graphic representation may, in the final analysis, be rooted in a much deeper transformation of values. It is the nature of the individual, of identity as a sustained act of privacy, and the relationship of the individual to the fact of death which may be altering profoundly as we move out of the middle-class phase of Western history. The criteria of private sensibility, of literary survival, as they are implicit in post-Renaissance poetry and fiction, of a literate exchange between writer and reader, may belong to a receding, perhaps inevitably élitist past. The collective, cinematic future, the new codes of indifference now developing in regard to individual death or artistic fame, may render obsolete the conventions of literature as we have known them. These questions arise directly from any consideration of eros and idiom, but go far beyond it.

At the present juncture it would appear that 'total emancipation' has in fact brought a new servitude, that literature, and especially prose fiction, is less free, less confident than it was. The collapse of taboos has led to a frenetic search for new shocks, for extremes of speech or behaviour as yet unexploited.

This is an unfashionable view. And I reject — though very uneasily when it comes to sadistic writing — any form of imposed censorship. But one contemporary master, at least, is in favour of censorship, precisely on grounds of poetic freedom. Jorge Luis Borges writes:

> In distinction from mathematical or philosophical language, the language of art is indirect; its essential, most necessary instruments are illusion and metaphor; not explicit declaration. Censorship impels writers to use procedures which are of the essence. . . . A writer who knows his craft can say all he wishes to say without affronting the good manners or infringing the conventions of his time. One knows full well that language itself is a convention.[1]

The question is a difficult one, and censorship only a minor aspect. What is at stake is the education, the quickening of human feelings as against their diminution through simplification and brutality. Because it lies at the heart of consciousness, sexual experience offers both a denial and a challenge to the genius of language. It is through that genius that men have, at least until now, principally defined their humanity.

[1] Jorge Luis Borges, 'Pornographie et censure', in *L'Herne* (Paris, 1964).

6

Whorf, Chomsky, and the Student of Literature
1974

The two positions we are considering can be termed 'monadist' or 'relativist', and 'universalist'. The monadist case holds that differences between languages outweigh similarities. That all men known to man use language in some form, that all languages of which we have evidence are able to name perceived objects or to signify action – these are undoubted truths. But belonging to the type 'all members of the species require oxygen to sustain life', they do not illuminate except in the most abstract, 'trivially deep' sense the actual workings of human speech. What matters are the fantastic diversities of grammatical form and semantic habit, what demands explanation is a complex but manifest history of centrifugal development. Our condition is, both obviously and in essence, that of mutual incomprehensibility after Babel. Between four and five thousand tongues are current on the earth. Several thousand more are known to have been spoken in the past. Any insight into the phenomenology of language must start from this enigmatic largesse and, finally, come back to it.

The universalist position asserts that the underlying structure of all languages is the same and thus common to all men. Dissimilarities between human tongues are essentially of the surface. Deep-seated structures and constraints generate and determine the forms of all grammars however singular or bizarre certain surface features seem to be. What is important is the understanding and formalization of these central generative elements; surface study is of primarily phonetic or historical interest.

Between these two poles of argument, there can be and

there are numerous intermediary, qualified approaches. Neither position is maintained very often with absolute rigour. There are 'monadic' touches and nuances of linguistic relativism in the universalist grammars of Roger Bacon, of the grammarians of Port Royal, and even in the contemporary transformational generative grammars. There are, on the other hand, universalist notions in the relativism of Humboldt, of Sapir, and even of Whorf.

In their modern guise, moreover, both great lines of argument may be traced to a common source.

In 1697, in his tract on the amelioration and correction of German, Leibniz put forward the all-important suggestion that language is not the vehicle of thought but its determining medium. Thought is language internalized and we feel and think as our particular language impels and allows us to do. Tongues differ even more profoundly than do nations. They also are monads, 'perpetual living mirrors of the universe' each of which reflects or, as we would now put it, 'structures' experience according to its own particular sight-lines and habits of cognition. No two languages construe the same world. Yet, at the same time, Leibniz shared many of the universalist aims and hopes which had been, since Bacon's plea for a 'real character' in the *Advancement of Learning* of 1605, so typical a strain in seventeenth-century thought. To the end of his life, Leibniz made suggestions toward a universal semantic system, immediately legible to all men. Such a system would be analogous to mathematical symbolism, so efficacious precisely because the conventions of mathematics are grounded in the very fabric of human reason and are, therefore, independent of any local variation. A *characteristica universalis* would be analogous also to Chinese ideograms. Once a 'world catalogue' had been agreed to, all messages could be deciphered instantaneously whatever the native speech of the recipient and the disaster at Babel would, on the graphic level at least, be mended.

A comparable coexistence of monadist and universalist concepts may be found in Vico. Philology is the key to the *Scienza nuova* because a study of the evolution of speech faculties is a study of the evolution of mind. Metaphor, especially, is a universal factor in man's acquisition of active sensibility and cultural self-awareness. All nations most probably traverse the same major phases of linguistic usage, from the immediate and sensory to the abstract. Simultaneously, however, Vico's opposition to Descartes and to the extensions of Aristotelian logic in Cartesian rationalism made of him the first true 'linguistic historicist' or relativist. Though all men sought expression through 'imaginative universals' (*generi fantastici*), these universals rapidly acquired very different configurations. 'Almost infinite particulars' make up both the syntactic and lexical corpus of different tongues. These particulars engender and reflect the strikingly diverse world-views of races and cultures. The degree of 'infinite particularity' reaches so deep that a universal 'logistic' or grammar of language of the Aristotelian or Cartesian mathematical model is fatally reductionist.

It is doubtful that Vico really influenced Hamann. Kabbalistic speculations and the pregnant muddle of Hamann's remarkable intellect were obviously more important. But whatever the immediate background, Hamann's *Versuch über eine akademische frage* of 1760 marks the decisive move towards a relativistic language theory. It is of little importance that Hamann erroneously ascribed linguistic differences to imperceptible variations in the speech organs of different races. The suggestive strength of his theories lies in the axiom that each language is an 'epiphany' or articulate embodiment of a specific historical-cultural landscape. Hebrew verb forms are inseparable from the intricate niceties of Jewish ritual. But Hebrew has itself shaped and determined what it reveals as being the specific genius of a community. The process is dialectical, with the formative energies of language moving both inward and outward in a civilization.

Despite their turgid, rhapsodic manner, Hamann's *Vermischte Anmerkungen* (1761) and *Philologische Einfälle und Zweifel* (1772) are, so far as I know, the first serious applications of relativist principles to the study of actual languages. Examining the differing lexical and grammatical resources of French and German, Hamann argues that neither Cartesian coordinates of general, deductive reasoning nor Kantian mentalism can account for the creative, 'pre-rational' and manifold proceedings through which language — unique to the human species but exceedingly varied among nations — shapes reality (*Sprachgestaltung*) and is, in turn, shaped by local historical experience.

Though indebted to certain of Hamann's suggestions, Herder's work marks a transition to genuine comparative linguistics. Calling for 'a general physiognomy of the nations from their languages', Herder asserted that national character-istics are 'imprinted on speech' and, reciprocally, carry the stamp of the particular tongue. Where a language is corrupted or bastardized, there will be a corresponding decline in the temper and fortunes of the body politic. It is the pre-eminent task of the poet to ensure the vitality of his native speech.

The short years between Herder's writing and those of Wilhelm von Humboldt were among the most productive in the history of linguistic thought. Sir William Jones's celebrated *Third Anniversary Discourse on the Hindus* of 1786 initiated modern Indo-European philology. Schlegel's *Ueber die Sprache und Weisheit der Indier* (1808) helped to disseminate Jones's ideas and did much to establish the concepts of com-parative grammer. In 1813, Mme de Staël's *De l'Allemagne* gave wide currency to the theory that there were crucial, formative interactions between a language (in this case, German) and the history, political institutions, and psychology of a people. All these directions of argument and conjecture seem to come together in the work of Humboldt.

Humboldt's achievement is too central and well-known to require more than a brief summary. It includes the January 1822 lecture *Ueber das Entstehen der grammatischen Formen und ihrem Einfluss auf die Ideen Entwicklung*, and the magnum opus on which Humboldt was engaged from the 1820s until his death in 1835: *On the Differentiation of the Structure of Human Language, and its Influence on the Spiritual Evolution of the Human Race*. Language is the only verifiable and *a priori* framework of cognition. Our perceptions result from the imposition of that framework on the total, unorganized flux of sensations. 'Die Sprache ist das bildende Organ des Gedankens,' says Humboldt, using both *bildend* and *Bildung* in their forceful, twofold connotation of 'image' and 'culture'. Different linguistic frames define different world-images. 'Every language is a Form and carries in itself a Form-Principle. Each has a unity consequent on the inherent, particular Principle.' So far as each human tongue differs from every other, the resulting shape of the world is a local selection from a total but random potentiality. In this way, Humboldt conjoins the environmentalism of Montesquieu and the nationalism of Herder with an essentially post-Kantian model of human consciousness as the active and diverse shaper of the perceived world.

Ueber die Verschiedenheit des menschlichen Sprachbaus (particularly Sections xix and xx) is crowded with linguistic ideas of prophetic brilliance. It can be shown to anticipate both C.K.Ogden's theory of 'opposition' and the binary structuralism of Lévi-Strauss. But the heart of the argument lies in its application to actual linguistic-cultural material.

Humboldt sets out to correlate Greek and Latin grammar

with the histories and social character of the two respective civilizations. Greek syntax casts a finely-woven net of relations over the currents of life. Hence the diacritical genius of Greek thought and poetry. Hence also the atomizing, divisive quality of Greek political life and its vulnerability to the tempting ambiguities of sophistry. The sobriety, the laconic idioms, the inbuilt masculinity of Latin are the active mould of the Roman way of life. And so on.

The presentation is eloquent and acute in its treatment of historical details: but it is circular. Civilization is uniquely and specifically informed by a given language; that language is the unique and specific matrix of its civilization. The one proposition is used to demonstrate the other and vice versa. Given the final mystery of creative relation between *Sprache* and *Geist*, it could hardly be otherwise. But this circularity will continue to be the weakest aspect of the relativist position.

There is no need here to do more than indicate the lines of continuity from Humboldt to Whorf. Via the work of Steinthal (the editor of Humboldt's fragmentary texts), linguistic relativity enters the anthropology of Franz Boas. From there it reaches the ethno-linguistics of Sapir and Whorf. A parallel movement takes place in Germany. Cassirer's doctrine of the unique 'inner form' which distinguishes a particular tongue from all others, derives immediately from Humboldt's *Form-Prinzip*. In a series of books written between 1929 and 1950, Leo Weisgerber sought to apply the 'monadic' principle to actual, detailed investigations of German syntax and of the intellectual and psychological attitudes which that syntax has generated and embodied in German history. During the 1930s, Jost Trier developed his theory of 'the semantic field'. Each tongue or language-monad 'diffuses' and operates inside the shell of a total conceptual field (the imagistic correlations with quantum physics are obvious). In each case the linguistic feedback from experience is a particular one. Speakers of different languages thus inhabit different 'mediary worlds' (*Zwischenwelten*).

Edward Sapir's formulation, in an article dated 1929, summarizes the entire line of argument as it goes back to Leibniz:

The fact of the matter is that the 'real world' is to a large extent unconsciously built up on the language habits of the group. No two languages are ever sufficiently similar to be considered as representing the same social reality. The worlds in which different societies live are distinct worlds, not merely the same world with different labels attached.

Our customs of speech are the outcome of a cumulative dialectic of differentiation; languages generate different social forms, these forms further divide languages.

The work of Benjamin Lee Whorf can be seen as an extention and refinement of Sapir's statement. Whorf's 'metalinguistics' are currently under severe attack by both linguists and ethnographers. But the papers gathered in *Language, Mind and Reality* (1956) constitute a model and methodology of understanding which has extraordinary elegance and philosophic tact. They are a statement of vital possibility relevant not only to the linguist and anthropologist but also to the poet and student of literature. Whorf had something of Vico's philosophic curiosity. The years in which he, Roman Jakobson, and I.A.Richards are active simultaneously count among the key moments in the history of the formal penetration of consciousness.

Whorf's theses are well known. The native tongue of an individual determines what he perceives of the world and how he thinks/feels about it. Each language constructs its own 'thought world' made up of 'the microcosm which each man carries about within himself, by which he measures and understands what he can of the macrocosm.' There is no 'universal objective reality', only an aggregate of 'segmentations' made by different language-cultures. This does *not* mean (Whorf is often misconstrued on this issue) that there are not rudimentary universal neuro-physiological apprehensions of time, space, identity, and sequence common to the human species. But these universals ramify and take on local specification as soon as the infant enters the world of his particular speech. Thus there is a distinctive Indo-European time-sense and a corresponding system of tense. Different 'semantic fields' divide the total spectrum of colours, sounds, and scents in very different ways (the only universal would be that of organic limitation). Whorf sums up his vision in one of his last papers:

Actually, thinking is most mysterious, and by far the greatest light upon it that we have is thrown by the study of language. This study shows that the forms of a person's thoughts are controlled by inexorable laws of pattern of which he is unconscious. These patterns are the unperceived intricate systemizations of his own language—shown readily enough by a candid comparison and contrast with other languages, especially those of a different linguistic family. His thinking itself is in a language—in English, in Sanskrit, in Chinese. And every language is a vast pattern-system, differing from others, in which are culturally ordained the forms and categories by which the personality not only communicates, but also analyzes nature, notices or neglects types of relationship and phenomena, channels his reasoning, and builds the house of his consciousness.

To show that this thesis 'stands on unimpeachable evidence' Whorf was prepared to apply comparative semantic analyses to Latin, Greek, Hebrew (there are notably links between his own work and the theosophic Kabbalism of Fabre d'Olivet), Kota, Aztec, Shawnee, Russian, Chinese, and Japanese. But it is Whorf's work on the Hopi languages of Arizona, in a series of key papers written between ca.1935 and 1939, which counts most. It is here that the notion of interactive 'pattern-systems' of life and language is argued from specific, detailed example.

Though only the expert is qualified to deal with these analyses, Whorf's conclusion is famous and arresting enough to be worth restating. The metaphysical framework imposed by Hopi grammars is far better suited than that of English to the world-picture of modern science. The Hopi treatment of events, inferential reasoning, and 'action at a distance' is, according to Whorf, delicate and susceptible of provisional postures in just the way required by twentieth-century wave-particle theory or relativity physics.

Whorf was tireless in emphasizing the built-in bias, the axiomatic arrogance of any theory of language based on very few tongues or on a scarcely veiled presumption that Sanskrit, Latin, or English constitute the natural, let alone optimal typology of all human speech. A picture of language, mind, and reality based almost exclusively on Cartesian-Kantian logic and on the semantic conventions of SAE (Standard Average European) is, argues Whorf, a hubristic simplification. The close of 'Science and Linguistics', a paper published in 1940, is worth quoting in full — especially at a time when the study of language in the United States is so largely dominated by an orthodoxy of confident generality and mathematical certitude:

A fair realization of the incredible degree of diversity of linguistic system that ranges over the globe leaves one with an inescapable feeling that the human spirit is inconceivably old; that the few thousand years of history covered by our written records are no more than the thickness of a pencil mark on the scale that measures our past experience on this planet; that the events of these recent milleniums spell nothing in any evolutionary wise, that the race has taken no sudden spurt, achieved no commanding synthesis during recent milleniums, but has only played a little with a few of the linguistic formulations and views of nature bequeathed from an inexpressibly longer past. Yet neither this feeling nor the sense of precarious dependence of all we know upon linguistic tools which are themselves largely unknown need be discouraging to science but should, rather, foster that humility which accompanies the true scientific spirit, and thus forbids that arrogance of the mind which hinders real scientific curiosity and detachment.

It is this kind of statement, added perhaps to I.A. Richards's observation that the translation of a Chinese philosophic text into English constitutes the 'most complex event' yet in the history of man, which the student of literature may wish to bear in mind when he thinks of his raw material — language.

Such is the assertive reach of Whorf's position that critiques of it, *per se*, make up a fair statement of the universalist case. 'There is no cogent reason to assume', writes E.H.Lenneberg 'that the grammarian's articulation of the stream of speech is coterminous with an articulation of knowledge or the intellect.' Words do not embody invariant mental operations. Any operational model of the linguistic process, i.e. Wittgenstein's finding that 'the meaning of a word is its use in the language,' will refute Whorf's primitive and deterministic parallelism of thought and speech. Moreover, if the Sapir-Whorf hypothesis were correct, if languages were indeed monads with essentially disparate meanings of reality, how then could we communicate interlingually? How could we acquire a second language or traverse into another language-world by means of translations? Yet, manifestly, these transfers do occur.

To the twelfth-century relativism of Pierre Hélie, with his belief that the catastrophe at Babel had generated as many kinds of irreconcilable grammars as there are languages, Roger Bacon opposed his axiom of fundamental unity: 'Grammatica una et eadem est secundum substantiam in omnibus linguis, licet accidentaliter varietur.' Without a *grammatica universalis* there can be no hope of genuine communication among peoples, nor any rational science of language. The accidental, historically moulded differences between tongues are, no doubt, striking. But underlying these there are principles of constraint, of invariance, of articulate relation which govern the character of all human speech. All languages known and conceivable are, says Noam Chomsky, 'cut from the same pattern'. Thus the true job of linguistics 'must be to develop an account of linguistic universals that, on the one hand, will not be falsified by the actual diversity of languages and, on the other, will be sufficiently rich and explicit to account for the rapidity and uniformity of language learning, and the remarkable complexity and range of the generative grammars that are the product of language learning.'

These universals may be phonological. As Trubetskoy and Jakobson have shown, the neuro-physiological equipment with which we emit and receive sounds is reflected in the acoustic structures of all human speech forms. Grammatical universals go deeper. They bear, for instance, on the ordering of subject-verb-object combinations and suggest that 'verb-object-subject' and 'object-verb-subject' are so rare as to constitute an eccentric violation of a universal sequence of perception. Other grammatical universals concern points of detail: 'when the adjective follows the noun, the adjective expresses all the inflectional categories of the noun. In such cases the noun may lack overt expression of one or all of these categories.' Drawing on thirty languages, J.H.Greenberg has listed forty-five fundamental grammatical relations which underlie all systems of human speech and which organize an essentially unitary picture of reality.

Chomskian grammar starts from dissatisfaction with the 'soft-edged' material of phonology and the superficiality of any ethno-linguistic, statistical treatment of grammatical universals. It proceeds to much greater phenomenological depths with its scheme of 'deep structures' which via a set of rules generate, i.e. 'bring to the surface', the sentences or 'phonetic events' which we actually speak and hear. The surface aspects of all languages, however divergent they may seem from each other, obey the same ultimate constraints and transformational procedures. Located 'far beyond the level of actual or even potential consciousness', these deep structures can be thought of as patterns of relation or strings of an order of abstraction far greater than even the most formal of grammatical rules. 'There is no reason to expect,' says Chomsky, 'that reliable operational criteria for the deeper and more important theoretical notions of linguistics . . . will ever be forthcoming.' Try to bring the creature to the light from the immense deeps of the sea and it will disintegrate or change form utterly. Yet some recent theories of universal grammar would go even deeper. Speaking of 'deep deep structures', Professor Emmon Bach suggests that Chomsky may be guilty of superficiality in comparing deep structures, even by analogy, with 'atomic facts' of grammatical relation. What we may be dealing with at this final level of instrumental universality are 'abstract kinds of pro-verbs which receive only indirect phonological representation' (in which I take 'pro-verbs' to signify potentialities of order 'anterior to' any conceivable rudiments of grammatical form).

But at whatever degree of depth we take it, generative grammar on the Chomskian model is universalist. It 'expresses directly the idea that it is possible to convey any conceptual content in any language, even though the particular lexical items available will vary widely from one language to another — a direct denial of the Humboldt-Sapir-Whorf hypothesis in its strongest form.'

Which of the two hypotheses is right?

As soon as one puts the question in this way, its crudity is apparent. Yet it is a crudity inherent in a good many of the claims of total insight and definitive verification put forward by transformational generative grammarians at this time. It may be a banal move, but of some heuristic use, to suggest that no single hypothesis of origin and structure will at one go elucidate the most complex phenomenological experience known to man, which is language. The probabilities against the finality of a single approach are increased by the fact that any model of the generation of human speech necessarily involves areas of molecular biology, neuro-physiology, anthropology and, possibly, 'archaeo-sociology' in which no single disciple has general competence.

Both the relativist and the universalist cases are open to serious question.

The circularity of argument, which we noted with reference to Humboldt, applies also to Whorf. What 'outside' evidence would either confirm or falsify Whorf's contention that differences of cognition underlie the Apache's description of a spring as 'whiteness moving downward'? There is a latent tautology in the assumption that a native speaker perceives experience differently because he talks about it differently — an assumption based on the fact that we deduce these differences of perception from those of speech. If genuine typologies of cognition and perception are involved, moreover, how is it that the Hopi or African speaker can communicate with us and is able, though with manifest strain, to adjust quite rapidly to 'our world'? (Yet Whorf might ask whether we ever really get through to each other; does the native ever really adjust, or is that adjustment a psychological mask forced upon him by our economic and behavioural demands?)

The underlying problem is that of *translation* in the full sense. There is, I believe, no deeper problem in the theory of language nor any about which our thoughts ought to be more provisional and solicitous of dissent.

The monadist position, carried to its logical conclusion, holds that no complete acts of translation between different semantic fields are possible, that all translation is approximate and ontologically reductive of meaning. The matrix of feeling and associative context which energizes usage in any given tongue can be transferred into another idiom only partly, and by virtue of periphrastic and metaphrastic manœuvres which inevitably downgrade the intensity, the evocative means, the formal autonomy of the original. Poets have often felt this.

A universalist grammar will affirm the contrary. The 'inter-translatability' of all languages, the fact that no 'closed speech' has been found on earth, none that native informant and learner from outside cannot, albeit by long and arduous work, 'externalize', make-up one of the strongest universalist 'proofs'. But let us look closely at the argument as it is stated in Chomsky's *Aspects of the Theory of Syntax*:

The existence of deep-seated formal universals . . . implies that all languages are cut to the same pattern, but does not imply that there is any point by point correspondence between particular languages. It does not, for example, imply that there must be some reasonable procedure for translating between languages.

It is difficult to avoid the sense of a very important hiatus or *non-sequitur*.[1] A footnote reinforces one's perplexity: 'The possibility of a reasonable procedure for translation between arbitrary languages depends on the sufficiency of substantive universals. In fact, although there is much reason to believe that languages are to a significant extent cast in the same mould, there is little reason to suppose that reasonable procedures of translation are in general possible.'

What does this mean?

'Point to point' only obscures the logical and substantive issue. The 'topology' through which linguistic universals can be transferred from language to language — note the covert pressure in the phrase 'between arbitrary languages' — may lie

[1] Cf. the detailed discussion of this issue in G. Steiner, *After Babel* (Oxford, 1975).

very deep, but if it operates at all, a 'point by point' correspondence *at some level* must be demonstrable. In which case a 'reasonable procedure of translation' must, at least, be analytically describable. If, on the contrary, there is little reason to suppose that such a procedure is 'in general' possible (and what does 'in general' signify?), what true evidence have we of universal structures? Could it be that the theory whereby transformational rules map semantically interpreted 'deep structures' into phonetically interpreted 'surface structures' is a meta-mathematical idealization of great elegance and logical reach, but not a picture of natural language?

The lacuna between the assumption of universal deep structures and any 'reasonable procedure for translation' is a serious one. Quine's treatment of the indeterminacies of translation in Chapter Two of *Word and Object* probably comes as close as any we have to putting this immensely difficult topic into focus. Significantly, Quine's analysis has aspects that can be called Whorfian and an analytic framework which is nearer to Chomsky. And incisive as it is, Quine's discussion is far from being a solution to the problem of what it is that occurs, of what formal and existential moves are performed, when a speech act crosses from one language to another.

Obviously the critical test for the two approaches lies in their application to the study of actual languages. As Chomsky himself says, what is needed is 'serious comparative work that tries to operate in the only logically appropriate way, namely, by constructing descriptive adequate grammars of a variety of languages and then proceeding to determine what universal principles constrain them, what universal principles can serve to explain the particular form that they have.' He cites Hugh Matthews's grammar of Hidasta, Paul Postal's work on Mohawk, Ken Hale's studies of Papago and Walbiri, and several other studies as cases in point. Though only the ethnolinguist in the relevant field can judge, there is no reason to doubt Chomsky's estimate of these monographs. The difficulty arises over what is meant by the construction of a 'descriptively adequate grammar'. Whether we have such a grammar for Latin, let alone English, is a moot point. There are logicians and linguists who are convinced that no set of rules, however complete, is sufficient to describe the utterances possible in any living language, and that the notion of such description being made adequately by an outsider to the ethnic, cultural, historical milieu is entirely unrealistic.

At the same time, it is worth emphasizing that the issues raised by Whorf and the methods he initiated are far from being exhausted or refuted. Lines of work first sketched at the 1953 conference on 'Language in Culture' are still in progress. It is far too early to tell whether the solution to undoubted problems of differentiation between cultures and conceptual conventions lies in the fact, urged by Franklin Fearing among others, that the earth is peopled by communities at very different stages of evolution. In relation to the total number of spoken languages, our studies remain statistically almost insignificant. 'It is still premature to expect,' says one linguist, 'that we can make any except the most elementary observations concerning linguistic universals and expect them to be permanently valid. Our knowledge of two-thirds or more of the world's languages is still too scanty (or in many instances non-existent).' As Helmut Gipper concludes, in what is the most balanced assessment made so far of Whorf's theses, these theses are, in their initial form, inadequately supported and methodologically vulnerable. But the questions posed by Whorf are of the utmost importance to the understanding of language and of culture.[1] The jury is still out.

[1] See Helmut Gipper, *Bausteine zur Sprachinhaltsforschung* (Düsseldorf, 1963) pp.297–366.

Perhaps I may be allowed one further quotation. It sets the debate between relativists and universalists in its philosophic context: 'In the light of the foregoing considerations,' says Max Black in his paper on 'Language and Reality', 'the prospects for a universal philosophical grammar seem most unpromising. I believe the hope of finding *the* essential grammar to be as illusory as that of finding the single true co-ordinate system for the representation of space. We can pass from one systematic mode of spatial representation to another by means of rules for transforming co-ordinates and we can pass from one language to another having the same fact-stating resources by means of rules of translation. But rules for transformation of co-ordinates yield no information about space; and translation rules for sets of languages tell us nothing about the ultimate nature of reality.'

As we step back from the immediate topic of universals, it becomes readily apparent that nothing less is involved than a view of the fundamental realities of language. At bottom, the controversy between transformational generative theories and other approaches turns on the question as to whether or not languages are well-defined or ill-defined systems. These two terms have exact mathematical and philosophical meanings and entailments. A Chomskian analysis of deep structures and re-write rules is based on the working hypothesis that language is a well-defined system. 'What we scholars have learned about language in the course of a hundred and fifty years of backbreaking work,' counters Hockett, 'persuades me that language is an ill-defined system, and that it is part of the total physical human experience that has made it possible for man to invent well-defined systems in the first place.'

It is improbable that this disagreement, rooted as it is in much more ancient epistemological conflicts over nominalism and realism, will ever be resolved by any unitary, demonstrable solution. Alternative mappings and orderings of major phenomenologies (i.e., language) do not cancel each other out. And where even the acutest of linguistic philosophers fears to tread — remember Austin's modest goal of doing no more than augmenting the 'sensitivity of our awareness of ordinary language usage' — the student of literature will be doubly hesitant.

Yet in fact, he has made his choice. This is my main point. Wherever and whenever we are studying a literary text, we have chosen as between a Whorfian and a Chomskian methodology. Whether we trouble to define such frameworks for ourselves or not, our perceptions of language *in literature* are relativist and, if the term may be allowed, *ultra-Whorfian*.

When we investigate the history of a language, when we read a poem or piece of prose with full response, we are implicated in a matrix of inexhaustible specificity. The more we get on with the job, the more enmeshed we are in an experience of irreducibly complex, singular life-forms.

The sources of this specificity are various. The student of literature sees language diachronically. He knows that the pressures of time are incessant and intricate. A speech act is embedded in the conventions, social and philosophic inferences, contingent emphases of the moment. The armature of locution, the way in which a proposition is hinged and pressed home in, say, a poem of the 1720s differs markedly from what would be current only fifteen years later. The permanence of major literature is paradoxically time-bound. Indeed it is inside literature that linguistic change, the development of new tonalities, the transformations of the semantic field, are most salient. As our antennae grow less blunt, we come to know that poetry, drama, fiction, the essay, are the calendar of language and that a year — 1798, 1836, 1924 — can bring on changes whose complexity and reach our best means of analysis fail to exhaust.

Another source of uniqueness is that of location. Language varies from place to place, sometimes from borough to borough. It carries the manifold impress of the social and professional milieu. There is an idiom above and below stairs, an argot in the ghetto and a *lingua franca* of the market place. The circumstantial pressures on speech are, in a strict sense, immeasurably diverse, and literature embodies that plurality.

Let me argue the point in a heightened, over-simplified way: there is not a significant literary text — it may be quite short — which does not generate its own 'language-sphere', whose bare existence will not, if we choose to experience it fully, somewhat alter the field of recognitions, the associative fabric, of the rest of language. The apprehension of literature does not bear on universals but on 'ontological particulars' (the term derives from Heidegger and from Heidegger's commentary on Hölderlin). The readiest example is that of the total work of a given writer. The performative acts by which a writer creates his recognizable 'world' are linguistic. The concept of 'style' is notoriously elusive but, when looked at seriously, comprises far more than an external treatment of certain aspects of language. A coherent style is a counter-statement to the collective, unexaminedly normative conventions of vision operative or, more precisely, residual and largely inert in the surrounding vulgate. It 'speaks its vision of things', and where that locution has scope and a logic of internal unfolding, we enter the writer's construct as we would a climate and a landscape in its singular light. But at all points, that new and 'signed' reality is generated by language, by the writer's use of a vocabulary and syntax grounded in the vulgate but refined, complicated, made new by intensity of personal statement.

Thus there is, in the strict sense, a lexicon and grammar for every serious work of literature. That we have such glossaries and grammars for Dante, Shakespeare, or Rabelais and not for most other writers is an accident of pre-eminence. Every writer of substance develops a 'language-world' whose contours, tonality, and idiosyncracies we come to recognize. And each is susceptible of lexical and grammatical investigation. Where Whorf finds that every language and the culture which that language articulates organizes (makes organic) its particular 'thought-world', the reader of literature will say the same of every writer and, where penetrative response is pressed home, of every major poem, play, or novel.

The difficulty lies in the bluntness, in the improvised character of what Coleridge called our 'speculative instruments'. It is not only that we know next to nothing about the anatomy of the inventive proceedings, about the translation of private feelings into public form, but that the elements of particularity which a work of literature offers to examination are formidably numerous, subtle, and interrelated. It is likely that they are, in the arithmetic and logical sense of the term, incommensurable.

The issue is straightforward but needs exact phrasing. The analytic modes which we can focus on a text are numerous and fairly well defined. They include the bibliographical, the philological, the historical, the psychological, the sociological, the biographic, and several more. Let us suppose that we have brought each of these 'readings' to bear, that there is no linguistic, formal, contextual aspect of the poem to which we have not applied the relevant discipline of elucidation. Yet invariably the sum of our understanding will fall short of the facts of meaning before us. If it were otherwise, our exegesis would produce an active tautology, a counterpart to the poem which would in every respect of significance be the equal of the original. But outside the fables of Borges there are no total meta- or para-phrases. The best reading, the best criticism will serve the poem or the play by making visible, by making analytically expressive, the distance which separates it from the object of its attention. A major exercise of understanding — Coleridge on the *Lyrical Ballads*, Mandelstam on the *Divina Commedia* — is one which circumscribes the original text with a scrupulously drawn circuit of inadequacy. It says to us: 'analysis, location, interpretative echo can go so far and no further.' But it says so in a manner that leaves the work itself more spacious, more autonomously lucid, and that leaves criticism stronger, more worth attempting and disagreeing over. The process is one of honestly argued distance and epistemological tact.

There is nothing mystical about the 'inexhaustibility' of the literary work. In part the reasons are contingent. We can never know enough of the precise etymological values of the writer's vocabulary, of the exact interplay between general currency and personal idiom at the moment in which the poem was written, of the sensibility, itself perhaps local and intimately inferred, to which the writer addresses himself on a given occasion. In a mature poem, novel, or drama the defining context of any element — stylistic, prosodic, phonetic — is the work as a whole. It could be shown that there is not a paragraph, perhaps not a sentence in *Madame Bovary* whose semantic values do not implicate the entirety of the book. This sort of dynamic cohesion is beyond the enumerative and dissociative scope of critical re-statement. But one can go further; the context of a great work of art is the sum of its culture, of the executive means that have gone before, of the works that will follow. There are no methodologically predicted limits of relevance. The total context of potential meaning is, in the Wittgensteinian sense, 'all that is the case.'

But there are also ontological grounds of irreducibility. The interaction of text and interpreter is never closed. The

very opaque concept of 'indeterminacy' in physics, the difficulties which stem from the ways in which observation acts
on that which is being observed, are a commonplace in our
experience of literature. No reading is neutral. The material
alters in what could be termed 'the field of force' set up by
the reader's demands and responses. The existentiality, the
histories of the *Odyssey,* of *Lear,* of *Les Fleurs du mal* are
made up, in substantial proportion, of all the readings and
misreadings which these texts have elicted and will elicit in
future. Our own sight-lines to the work change with different
personal circumstances, with age, and in relation to the open-
ended aggregate of whatever else we have read or experienced.
Both halves of the equation — the text and the act of reading
— are, as it were, in motion. That the classic work persists
enhanced and productively complicated by the accumulation of commentaries, imitations, pastiches, parodies, and
explications is one of the symptoms of major form (minor
work can be diminished by insight, it can become the equivalent or even the lesser occasion of the interpretations it gives
rise to).

   The upshot is that the order of complexity, the order of
relation between analysis and object as they occur in the
study of literature are generically beyond anything that can
be dealt with in linguistics. It is a matter of acute philosophical and technical controversy as to whether we have, until
now, achieved a *complete* description, a complete formalization of even the most elementary speech unit ('John loves
Mary'). It is, to put it modestly, less than plausible that such
analysis will be applicable to the literally open-ended
dynamics of even the simplest of literary texts.

   Does this mean that the critic and student of literature
have nothing to learn from linguistics? As I have tried to
shown, most recently in a set of papers on the two

approaches,[1] precisely the contrary is the case.

The kind of collaborative study of poetics, literary composition, style and genre, advocated by the Leningrad and Moscow 'Language Circles' at the start of the century, and later pursued in Prague, continues to be a vital current and necessary ideal. Simplistic, schematized as is their treatment of natural language, linguistic techniques nevertheless are of extreme interest to the 'reader in depth'. To a large extent, this is a matter of stance, of the quality of closeness and surprise which the linguistic analysis of syntax and semantics brings to the texture of statement. It is hardly possible to read the best of modern linguistics from, say, Saussure to Chomsky, or such linguistic philosophers as Moore, Austin, Quine, or Strawson without acquiring a more patient, critically tensed regard for the problem before one. Jakobson's famous plea that we see the grammar of poetry as a product of the 'poetry of grammar', i.e., the 'poetic resources concealed in the morphological and syntactic structure of language,' is no more than common sense. But the force of interrelation is, I think, heuristic and methodological; it is, in Austin's vein, a matter of keeping oneself more scrupulously off balance.

It we allow 'linguistics' to include ancillary disciplines such as 'ethno-linguistics' or linguistic anthropology, 'socio-linguistics' and the study of speech lesions and pathologies ('psycho-linguistics'), the extent of relevance to the history and criticism of literature becomes unmistakable. Dr. Leavis's admonition that 'language, in the full sense, in the full concrete reality . . . eludes the cognizance of any form of linguistic science,' is, if anything, too restrictive. It is by no means clear that there is, as yet, 'a linguistic science' as contrasted with a provisional aggregate of models and methodological trials. But 'language in the full sense' also eludes the

[1] G.Steiner, *Extraterritorial* (London and New York, 1971).

cognizance of all known techniques of critical, textual, historical penetration. What are hoped for are local gains, clarifications of the particular case, moves toward a more resilient, productive condition of disagreement. And in that respect the profit to be derived from a collaborative linguistic-critical approach is already visible.

We *do* read differently since Jakobson and I.A.Richards. We have a new intimation of the ways in which a literary work internalizes its criteria of coherence. We deal far more warily than did Dr.Johnson or Matthew Arnold with the vexed question of 'poetic truth', with the supposition that such practices as metaphor generate a system of 'truth-functions', a logic, properly speaking 'a symbolic logic', of their own. We benefit from a growing awareness of the inter-actions — cumulative, contradictory, dislocatory — between meaning and syntax in a literary style. A statistical analysis which shows that sound effects in Pope are likely to coincide with lexical meanings whereas in Donne there is a discord-ance, probably intentional, between phonetic effects and semantic units, is more than ingenuity. It may induce funda-mental insights about the differences in the relations of feelings to expressive means as between Metaphysical and Augustan poetics. It is difficult to suppose that Austin's work on the 'illocutionary force of utterance' in speech-acts, and the grammatical-philosophic discussions which have arisen from it, will be of no interest to our understanding of dramatic verse, of dialogue in fiction, of vocative structures in rhetoric. Such examples can be multiplied.

Already, there have been at least two movements in literary study that embody the stimulus and controls of linguistics. The first would include the work of Spitzer, of Curtius, and much of Jakobson. It represents a conjunction of stylistic and historical concerns with comparative philology and dia-chronic *Sprachwissenschaft* in the traditional sense. Via

Jakobson, Richards, and Empson, these traditional comparative approaches modulate towards the new, more technically
oriented language-consciousness of modern semantics,
linguistic philosophy and deep-structure. The dual focus of
literary-linguistic grasp which has produced Empson's
Structure of Complex Words, Donald Davie's two incisive
books on energy and structure in English verse, Tzvetan
Todorov's analyses of epic narrative, Roland Barthes on
Balzac, Josephine Miles's 'More Semantics of Poetry', or
Archibald Hill's 'Poetry and Stylistics', to name a few, will
not be readily ignored. Indeed, there is ground for supposing
that the future of literary studies and of certain important
aspects of criticism lies in a developing relation to linguistics.
The latter will, I would judge, form an increasing part of the
backbone of discipline and acquired competence in the
university curriculum in literature.

But the relation can be fruitful only if the respective
orders of concern are clearly understood. What stands in the
way of this essential discrimination is the current usage of
the terminology of 'depth' and 'surface' or, more exactly,
the entailment of hierarchy which these terms carry with
them.

By definition, the reader and student of literature work 'at
the surface'. They deal with the phonetic facts, the words
and sentences as we can actually see and hear them. That is
the only reality available to us. Is there any other? Transformational generative grammars assure us that there is, that the
articulate presence of the text is merely the external, partly
contingent product of generation out of deep and primal
structures. What are these structures like? Are they neuro-
physiological or even molecular in nature? Are they in some
way 'imprinted' on the evolving cortex? Do they constitute
a kind of 'presyntactic' holograph of an order of abstraction
and formalization beyond anything we are able to describe?

The Chomskian theory of language gives no answers. At times, Chomsky suggests that it is entirely unrealistic to believe that any answer will ever be forthcoming. At other points, as in the often acrimonious exchanges on innate ideas, he seems to hint at a more traditional, meta-Kantian scheme of mentalism and 'programming'.

But whatever its opaqueness and unexamined metaphoric content, the notion of 'deep structure' conveys a powerful positive valuation and that of 'surface' is inherently pejorative. Yet it may be that this whole axis of verticality, with its strong symbolic inferences, is spurious. As we have seen, the 'surface' of language is inexhaustibly complex. Here surface has nothing qualitatively, ontologically superficial. The idiomatic, historical, contextual, personal parameters which energize spoken and written speech are diverse and changing beyond any available analytic reduction. And they have their own genuine 'depths'. In the actual history of a word or phrase, time has a fantastically complex life of previous echo. Deep planes of social evolution, perhaps of kinetic and neuro-psychological adjustment, underlie prosodic modes in verse and the less visible but operative stress systems of prose. Whether or not psychoanalytic investigations have offered verifiable insights into the creative process, whether their elucidations of image and symbol are valid, remains an open question. But there can be no doubt as to the realities of depth which relate the presence of the poem to the nascent purpose of the writer. These relations, like the invention of melody, are among the most complex phenomena of which we have any, albeit the most rudimentary, cognizance.

We must discriminate between uses of 'deep'. The tree-structure of diagrams which spangle the pages of current readers in transformational generative grammar are *not* an x-ray. They do *not* give a 'picture in depth' in any empirical, independently verifiable sense. They are themselves an argumentative device, a graphic presentation of a particular hypothesis about language and mind. That hypothesis may or may not prove valid. And even if it should prove valid, the result may be a 'trivial depth'. That is to say: the discoveries made about grammatical structure and universals may prove to be applicable only to elementary, arbitrarily schematized units, or they may prove to be of an unexceptional but banal generality such as the proposition that all grammars include some form of quantifiers. This possibility of 'trivial depth' is a key one. The inexhaustible, elegant, mentally taxing profundities of chess offer a fair analogy.

The 'depths' with which we are confronted in our study of literature are, by contrast, messy, ill-defined, and individuated. But they are not trivial. There is, from the point of view of the reader, of the critic, more insight into the generation of language in the letters of Keats or in Nadezhda Mandelstam's account of her husband's methods of composition — the lips under compulsion of inchoate music before the shadowy 'ascent to words' — than can be found in any linguistic treatise. Which is as it should be. Both approaches are concerned with the overriding fact of human speech. But the areas of inquiry and the degree of precision aimed at differ significantly.

'Wanted: An Ontological Critic' advertised John Crowe Ransom in 1941. If that phoenix turns up he will, I expect, be part linguist. What I have wanted to suggest is that his linguistics — so far as they bear on the autonomous life-forms of the poem — will be, uneasily, Whorfian. Ours must remain, as Blake said, 'the holiness of minute particulars'.

7

Dante Now: The Gossip of Eternity
1976

In his essay 'Talking About Dante', Osip Mandelstam compares the *Divina Commedia* to a crystallographic growth which the unceasing drive towards the creation of interlocking forms penetrates and unites.

Thus, one has to imagine how it would be if bees had worked at the creation of this thirteen-thousand-faceted shape, bees endowed with instinctive stereometric genius, who attracted more and still more bees as they were needed. The work of these bees, who always keep an eye on the whole, is not equally difficult at the various stages of the process. Their cooperation broadens and becomes more complex as they proceed with the formation of the combs, by means of which space virtually arises out of itself.

There is a comparable simile for dynamic coherence in Pope's *Essay on Man*:

> The spider's touch, how exquisitely fine!
> Feels at each thread, and lives along the line.

Crystals, honeycombs, the vital reticulations of the spider's web: each is an analogy towards Mandelstam's exultant find that the entirety of the *Commedia* 'is one single unified and indivisible stanza'. A stanza of 14,233 verses composed, so far as the evidence tells, over ten years of personal dislocation and political tumult. This live compaction, whose validation depends throughout on the quality of our reading, on our capacity, itself triggered and disciplined by the poem, to keep in reciprocal and equilibrating motion the overall design and the local intensity, obviously derives from several axes of relation ('one integral development of a crystallographic theme').

One axis is contextual. To cite a banal example (which may be best, inhibiting, as it does, the notion that one has something novel to contribute, yet showing, like the teasing ridge ahead of a mountain-walker, that there is always more perspective, more height to be worked for): the *Divina Commedia* has no direct knowledge of Homer. The Middle Ages draw their Homeric material from the compilation of the so-called Dictys Cretensis, in which Ulysses is done to death by Telegonus, his son by Circe. None the less, Dante is the only 'modern' (until Joyce) to have augmented fundamentally the reach of Homeric meaning, to have pierced to the core of that meaning by adding 'what was already there'. He is able to do so because the surrounding, sustaining literary-philosophic context is of an authority of suggestion and continuity so firm as to compel but also hold in place Dante's intuition of the Homeric sense. He visions the errant son of Laertes through a Latin perspective, through Virgil's own distancing and intimations of an archaic, lost excess of individual heroic stature — such vision through and past Virgil being at once the cognitive and the dramatic method of the *Commedia*'s concordance with the past.

In Book V of Cicero's *De finibus bonorum et malorum*, Dante finds a crucial gloss on the song of the Sirens. It was neither the sweetness of their voices nor the charm of their repertoire which riveted the passing voyager, but their profession of knowledge — *sed quia multa se scire profitebantur*. Little wonder, observes Cicero, that a man avid of intelligence (*mirum sapientiae cupido*) might prefer their solicitation even to a return home. Horace makes a comparable point in *Epistles* I, ii. The negative, which will be key to Dante's account of Ulysses' end, lurks, between the lines as it were, of Seneca's eighty-eighth moral letter, *Ad Lucilium*. The man, adverts Seneca, must have sailed outside our known world, *extra notum nobis orbem* (as the Genoese Vivaldi brothers were to do in 1291, disappearing without trace). We also, navigators on a daily, housebound scale, meet with fierce storms of the spirit, and our depravities thrust us into the proud miseries that afflicted Ulysses. A passing, almost casual moral *exemplum*, of the kind in which Seneca abounds, but nodal in the weave of reference and cross-reference.

There are further threads. Brunetto Latini, himself a talismanic figure of excellence and errancy in the *Inferno*, wrote a poem which told of the Pillars of Hercules where *la terra é terminata*. In Book I of the *Aeneid*, the hero exhorts his company to recall the dangers already past, and put away sad fear. The *Alexandreis* of the twelfth-century French poet Walter of Chatillon comes even closer; since there is nothing left of our world to traverse and lest our weapons go to rust, 'let us seek out those who dwell under another sun'. (Dante seems to have known this text.) The doomed vessel of his Ulysses spreads her wings exactly as did the argosies in *Aeneid* III, 520, and in verse 47 of Propertius' *Elegies* IV, vi. When fatality strikes, it does so in tested, licensed terms. The maelstrom at the foot of the Mountain of Purgatory closely resembles the vortex which spins and engulfs the ship in lines 114—17 of the first Book of the *Aeneid*. The murderous twist is the same and the words echo:

> ast illam ter fluctus ibidem torquet
> tre volte il fe' girar con tutte l'acque.

Dante's 'invention' in *Inferno* XXVI is prodigious, the narrative pace entirely his. But the mapping, the constraints which ensure depth yet contravene idiosyncracy and asymmetry, the charged economy of implication are contextual. They derive from the canonic availability of the classic precedent, from the axiomatic presupposition, without which the *Commedia* could literarlly not be, that all texts — poetic, fabulous, historical, mythographic, liturgical, philosophical, sacred, profane — are present for purposes of allusion and citation. The 'motion of spirit' (Dante's own phrase) which underwrites poetic craft is collective and cumulative. Context presses on text with the weight of shaping life, crystallizing particular inspiration, inhibiting extravagance which signifies waste wandering or autistic contrivance.

Another example. Canto XXV of the *Purgatorio* is among the most physiological and formally disputatious of the whole journey. The question, which Milton will remember, bears on the precise order of carnality to be attributed to the presence of the repentant dead ('how can they grow lean where there is no need of nourishment?'). Virgil replies by citing the extinction of Meleager as narrated in Book VII of Ovid's *Metamorphoses*. Here, too, there is a mystery of exact concurrence between seemingly unrelated entities — the wasting of a firebrand and the consumption of the wretched huntsman (a concurrence declared in one of the lapidary splendours of Latin poetry: *simul est exstinctus uterque*).

But the force of analogy is, to a precisely gauged degree, only partial and metaphoric. So Virgil calls on Statius to take up the argument. Statius is the lesser poet, a fact subtly pointed to by the 'prosaic' and technical character of his response. But his is a Christian soul whose access to revealed truths or, more exactly, to the logic of modulation from mundane to doctrinal patterns of understanding, is necessarily beyond that of Virgil. Statius' disquisition on digestion, on the metamorphic processes which connect nutriments to blood, blood to the generative virtues of the human organism, and these same virtues to the vegetative, sensitive and rational orders of the spirit, is at once dense and stringent. It draws, with the richly allusive economy made possible by the impartiality of the canonic, on a sequence of sources. These are both pagan and Christian, often in calculated alternation, and it is their mutual interrelations and cumulative mass which form a living framework (Mandelstam's hexagonal spaces 'virtually arising out of themselves'). There is Aristotle's *De generatione animalium*, Avicenna's *Canon* and *De animalibus*, Aristotle's *De anima,* Albertus Magnus' *De animalibus*, Averroës's commentary on the *De anima*. All these prefigure and are confluent in Aquinas's *Summa theologica* which teaches the ways and means of the transformation of spirits into spirit.

The adduction of authorities is far more than instrumental. The progress of understanding from Aristotelian intellection to Thomist certitude, via the privileged indirections of pagan and even Islamic conveyance, is re-enacted in the personal pilgrimage of the *Commedia*. The several and sequent apprehensions available to Virgil, Statius, and the Pilgrim who will proceed beyond Lethe to the conflagration of truth in which Albertus and Aquinas await him, illustrate, organize the ascent of intellect and imagination to revelation. But this revelation is latent, 'embryonic' in (an image directly intimated at different moments in this Canto) the inspired analytic labours of the ancients. Thus every facet of the poem relates to a relevant segment of the totality of preceding and contemporary literate expression, and this relation in turn cements, makes one, the fabric of the *Commedia*.

Another axis is that of local habitation and of names. Dante anchors spiritual motion and the ineffable in literal specificity. Spaces are densely material and topographical. In this way the primary meshing of text with context shades into the cognate category of 'texture', of the precise pliancies, rugosities, slipperiness or lapidary edge of matter. Rudolf Borchardt's uncanny 'translation' of the *Commedia* into archaic German (1904–30) captures this better than any commentary, making of the narrative a laboured voyage into concreteness, into mineshafts, marl-pits, rock galleries and up gritty moraines towards flares and crenellations of celestial light themselves strangely palpable.

Dante knew the ordnance-survey niceties of the Bible and their genius of suggestion. The *bolgia* in Canto XXX of the *Inferno* is 'eleven miles around and not less than half a mile across'; the visage of Nimrod in XXXI is as long as the celebrated bronze pine cone which stood originally near the Campus Martius (*i.e.* just over four yards high), and the giant measures *trenta gran palmi*, thirty full spans from the waist down. The width of the terrace in *Purgatorio* X is *misurrebbe in tre volte un corpo umano*, which signifies some 16 to 18 feet, using a module which even during the ascendant stages of disincarnation will remain that of the human figure. Such precisions, notably geometric, extend into the fiery heart of the *Paradiso*, setting up a crucial stylistic tension between concreteness and that which is by definition ineffable, unreproducible.

The voyage has a twofold mapping: internal and North Italian. The two are knit by a tactic of constant references. These are made to sites, often minute, in the Romagna, Tuscany, Lombardy, the Maremma. The titans in the pit of Hell are like the towers of Montereggioni, a castle on the crown of a low hill eight miles northwest of Siena. Antaeus bends his mighty bulk to pick up Virgil and Dante before depositing them in the final crucible of desolation. Pinpointing the colossus's gentle stoop, Dante compares it to the Garisenda, one of the leaning towers in Bologna, today 163 feet high and 10 feet out of perpendicular, 'when a cloud is passing over it against the direction in which it leans' (an added incisiveness and specification which shows Dante's tactile alertness to the play of light and air, of shadow and vapour against local stone). To make tangible the angles of ascent on the early screes of the Mountain of Purgatory, the Pilgrim cites the path to San Leo, perched on its rock-redoubt in the district of Montefeltro, and the dramatic tabular outcrop of Bismantova, some twenty miles south of Reggio in Emilia. In Canto XI of the *Paradiso* we are not far from the hem of pure fire and insubstantiality. But note how earth-rooted, circumstantial, Baedeker-like is Thomas's invocation of St. Francis: Assisi, the rivers Topino and Chiascio, the hills near Gubbio, the gentler, thus more fertile west slope of Mount Subasio, facing Perugia, and the Porta Sole from which one leaves Perugia for the high places. Exactitudes, pedantries, regionalisms which stabilise the leap of the visionary arc and posit authority.

Proper names cascade. The poet crams every rift of Hell and Purgatory with neighbours, enemies, literati, buggers, relatives, *condottieri*, property developers, lute-players. The silhouettes are often as sharply studied as in any novel, the discriminations hair-fine. The 'Spendthrift Brigade' of Siena, a circle of young gluttons, conspicuous consumers of wealth and their own persons, lodge now in hideous discomfort (covered with scabs, their nails running blood) near the nadir of damnation. Yet one of the crew, Lano of the Maconi family, is assigned to an entirely different quarter, the second *girone* of the seventh circle. It is we who cannot puzzle out the precise differentiation. Was it that Lano fell soldier-like in combat near Arezzo?

Or take the famous roll-call of Tuscan families, mostly extinct or grimly diminished, in *Purgatorio* XIV: da Valbona, Mainardi, Carpigna, Lambertazzi, Ubaldini, Tignosi, Traversari, Malvicini, Pagani — wolf-packs, patrons of the arts, lordlings of Bagnacavallo or Castrocaro, of Bertinoro or Forlì, lairs and parched hovels, *castelli* and marches, whose ferocious bustle can be traced in the quarterings of coats of arms, Villani's *Cronica* and Paget Toynbee's Dante dictionary. Again the unifying mechanism is one of compaction, of referential incrustation. The mad extremities of the infernal and the ever-loftier gradations towards disembodiment in the

Purgatorio are held in place by the prodigality and minuteness of local touch. We trust the teller's tale of the horrors in the thieves' *bolgia* (*Inferno* XXV) because of a pedantic but unforgettable nuance: Puccio Sciancato is tortured by the serpents but *non era mutato*, he alone has suffered no bodily change. A manuscript source recounts that, in distinction from his peers, this particular mafioso committed handsome, urbane thefts (*furti e legiardi*). He belonged to the Galigai family, Ghibellines banished in 1269. Ask anyone.

These nominations, moreover, establish time-coherence. The plural calendars of Dante's own biography, of the life of Beatrice (who dies in June of 1290), of the length of the journey, of the zodiac and of the historical temporalities which recede into the everlasting trajectories of Paradise, overlap, sometimes confusingly. The poet uses the arboreal continuity of families and clans to achieve unity. Often the same house reappears, fathers in Hell, sons in Purgatory, siblings divided between torment and beatitude, first cousins, in-laws flames or terraces apart. The pivot of the scheme is Dante's meeting with his great-great-grandfather in Canto XV of the *Paradiso*, and Cacciaguida's remembrance of times past. Once again the antique names sound: the Ravignani, the Nerli, the Alighieri themselves. The poem is made one ('a crystal-lographic shape, that is a body').

The technique and effect is exactly that of the narrator's return to the Guermantes salon, with its formal lament and ironies of recollection, name by name, misalliance, *arrivisme*, extinction heraldically charted, to circumscribe into a single organic mass the immensity of Proust's design. Indeed, the concurrences between the *Commedia* and the actual structure of *Le Temps retrouvé* would repay a close look. In both cases, precise trivia gather to a formidable persuasion. A motion of transcendence, of the internalization or negation of space and of time, is grounded in immanence, in the roughage and sensory ballast of locale, family scandal, coterie joke, parish idiom. The text is timeless, universal, because utterly dated and placed. Dante and Proust, like no others, give us the gossip of eternity.

A third trick of unison is self-evident: all of the *Commedia* echoes and cross-echoes. A covert but unmistakable allusion in line 132 of *Purgatorio* VI reveals to us that the towering peak which Ulysses glimpsed in *Inferno* XXVI is indeed the mountain-island of Purgatory. The Ithacan himself is invoked once again in those breath-stopping verses in Canto XIX of the *Purgatorio*:

> 'Io son,' cantava, 'io son dolce serena,
> che' marinari in mezzo mar dismago;
> tanto son di piacere a sentir piena!
> Io volsi Ulisse del suo cammin vago
> al canto mio; e qual meco s'aúsa,
> rado sen parte; si tutto l'appago!'

> ('I am,' she sang, 'I am the sweet Siren who leads mariners astray in mid-sea, so full am I of pleasantness to hear. Ulysses, eager to journey on, I turned aside to my song; and whosoever abides with me rarely departs, so wholly do I satisfy him.')

Dante kneels before the nearing angel in *Purgatorio* II precisely as he did in *Inferno* IX, 86–7. The oblique reference to Lethe in *Inferno* XIV, 136, will be cleared up only towards the close of the *Purgatorio* (XXVIII, 25–35). From the blessedness of *Paradiso* XI, the Pilgrim ponders the malign follies of men, of those who conduct their lives *per sofismi*. The turn of phrase is meant to recall to us Guido da Montefeltro's confession in Canto XXVII of the *Inferno*. And so on, individual words, elements of syntax, images, specific allusions and gestures chiming and echoing across the entire architecture of the poem in a pattern of responsions which, in its turn, acts out the principles of analogy and anagogy in Dante's interpretation of the world.

Add to this the formal bonds of prosody — the armature of Dante's terza rima allows every sort of placing: symmetrical, chiasmal, inverted, contrapuntal. Add to it also such ligaments as numerology (four for earth, three for the spiritual, twelve for apostles, zodiac, the months) and the mystique of literalism present in such pairings and mirrorings as *ave/Eva* — and you have some of the great axes of cohesion and convergent codes to account for Mandelstam's experience of 'stereometric genius', of a 'thirteen-thousand-faceted epic' which is one indivisible stanza.

These particulars can be harvested from Charles S.Singleton's new edition.[1] Six volumes, three of text, three of commentary, trim, chastely printed, flattering to the hand as are all Bollingen books. The Italian original, essentially that of Giorgio Petrocchi's *Edizione Nazionale* of 1966–8, is printed on the left and the English prose version on the facing page. Each in turn, *Inferno*, *Purgatorio* and *Paradiso*, has its attendant volume of line-by-line gloss, annotation, historical comment, citation of source and main parallels. The format is such that poem and elucidation can be taken in comfortably side by side. The exegesis is not, and is not meant to be, exhaustive. Picking up a volume at random, an Italian colleague pointed out to me that Singleton was perfectly right in quoting Ovid's *Metamorphoses* to show the provenance of one of the monsters in Hell, but that he omitted a passage in Ovid's *Fasti* from which one odd touch in the passage derives. There is an index of proper names but, damagingly, no précis of the kind provided by the old

---

[1] *The Divine Comedy: Inferno; Purgatorio; Paradiso*. Translated with a commentary by Charles S.Singleton. Bollingen Series LXXX. 6 vols. (Princeton, 1970–73).

Temple Classics. The bibliography is entirely philological and scholarly.

Indeed the note throughout is one of purism. Under 'modern commentators' one finds no T.S.Eliot, Ezra Pound, Osip Mandelstam, R.P.Blackmur or Francis Fergusson; no Erich Auerbach, Stefan George, Rudolf Borchardt or Philippe Sollers—poets, re-readers, exploiters who have helped the *Commedia* live at large. To Professor Singleton, who has expended a life-time on Dante, the maker of the poem has no match. His was the mind which came nearest of any to an authentic *mimesis* of 'God's created universe and of His providential plan for man and all creatures', an *imitatio* which must have been conceived in its manifold integrity from the very first verse of Canto I. There is still much to be cleared up from a contextual-linguistic point of view (a seventh volume of 'Danteana' is promised). But very likely, Professor Singleton would regard the notion of critical retrenchment or revaluation as fatuous.

The same spirit of ardent submission rules the translation. There are a good many English-language renditions available: Melville B. Anderson, J.D.Sinclair, the Dorothy Sayers–B.Reynolds enterprise, Laurence Binyon (which has more than its share of virtues), the Temple Classics by several hands. Material comparison with Singleton would be easy but pointless. He does not have the real translator's secret itch for parity. He would not offer an interposition, let alone a surrogate for the original. Singleton's is, in the best sense, a dignified trot, an interlinear mildly rounded and neutrally solemn in its cadences. It comes close to Walter Benjamin's paradox that the only great translations are primers, word-by-word interlinears, though the ideal which Benjamin adduces is, by hermetic perversion, Hölderlin's almost inaccessible Sophocles. Singleton's version is carefully inadequate and, therefore, heuristic. The reader is meant to piece out the

Italian for himself, using a dictionary and Dante grammar to guess more and more acutely, and leaning on the right-hand page when rescue or confirmation are needed. Professor Singleton's own stance is plain: anyone who is serious about the *Commedia*, which is the touchstone of the human perception of the rationale of mature existence, will take the trouble to trail after Dante in the 'noble vulgate.' The prose parallel in these volumes is only meant to be Limbo.

But will Professor Singleton's edition find its readers? Does the *Commedia*, even where it is decked out with a more ambitious traduction, imitation or counterpart?

It was with reference to Dante that T.S.Eliot, in 1929, sought to make verifiable the relations between a poet's religious or political doctrines and the reader's enjoyment of the work. Focused as it was on I.A.Richards's theory of 'pseudo-statements'—the sort of proposition which is true and persuasive in a given poetic matrix—and on his own motion towards a poetry of Anglican profession, Eliot's argument remains wobbly. One probably has more pleasure, he says, when one shares the poet's convictions. Dante's are of a subtlety and authority to provoke assent, where Shakespeare's often are not. Yet there is also 'a distinct pleasure' in responding to poetry whose systematic or implicit ideological content one does not accept. Dante caters to either or both of these possibilities. Somehow — and Eliot is both magisterial and shifty at this juncture — a fair amount of theological-philosophic matter has to be ingested. *In vacuo* disagreement or distaste would be puerile. But whatever one's personal reflex, the aspect of 'belief' or 'informed dissent' is crucial. Looking back, much of Eliot's worry strikes one as privileged. If we ask now 'who among us reads Dante, who is equipped to read him with immediacy, be it either of assent or rejection?', the answer may be less sheltered.

'Great literature is about LIFE': so goes the Lawrentian

cliché. Of course it is. But from the Middle Ages until our twentith-century neo-classics and ironic custodians (Eliot, Pound, Joyce, Mann, Valéry) this 'aboutness' has been intensely structured. It is an 'aboutness' which is itself mediate and literary in two principal ways. The writer in a high culture of received, challenged, unfolding genres will apprehend and filter fundamental responses to 'life' through other works. He does not stumble on experience raw. The latitudes and constraints which circumscribe the milieu of his invention, the provocations to metamorphosis, enlargement or critique which he will answer to, are 'there' already in the linguistic-literary lineage to which he belongs and which he may want to modify. The stylisation of reflexes can go so deep that the individual 'creator' is barely conscious of the fact that experience is reaching him via established conventions or 'sets' of aesthetic, technical precedent. (Gombrich has shown how Constable's sight of a particular bit of ground, presumably immediate and fully ocular to Constable himself, in fact derives from a Gainsborough treatment.) Vision is very often re-vision.

The second 'mediation' arises from the very notion of 'experience', 'reality' or 'raw material.' To many writers and thinkers, though not to all, another text is, or can be, the most naked and charged of life-forces. Such men live most intensely, most vulnerably, in the act of reading, in the shock of encounter with other poems, philosophic arguments, religious tracts, sometimes abstruse and remote in time. It makes no sense in such cases to divide 'brute experience' from experience already 'booked'. For innumerable revolutionaries the quintessential event of being, the epiphany, was the reading of Rousseau or of Marx. What locale, what physical and nervous happening, seemed to Shelley more life-transforming, more existential than a reading of Plato?

Dante is supremely 'bookish' in both senses. The relationship to Virgil, Ovid, Statius and Seneca, the exquisitely measured contiguities with or distances from Arnaut, Cavalcanti, Guinizzelli, are the stuff of his existence as man and as poet. Aristotle, Augustine, Aristotle through the sanctified glass of Aquinas, these are not 'sources' in any formal auxiliary way, but bodies of lived meaning, animate spaces of understanding and emotion in which Dante's sensibility registers its own pulse. Whatever the Middle Ages knew of classic and Hellenistic letters, of Greek, Roman and Islamic scientific-metaphysical doctrine, the entire corpus of patristic and canonic exegetics, the literature of the Provençal school and the 'new style' — all these are gathered into the *Commedia* at the most direct level of cerebral, nervous, sensory experience. The concept of allusion or analogue is totally inadequate. To Dante these other texts are the organic context of identity. They are as directly about life as life is about them.

Now it is just this fusion, this immersion in being and understanding via other texts, which we are ill equipped or inclined to handle. Fewer and fewer of us 'read' in Dante's sense of utter self-bestowal and re-vision. The post-romantic, post-Nietzschean scenario is one of untutored spontaneity, of impulses from the vernal wood outweighing libraries. The assumption that previous letters and philosophy can be decisive inscape (Hopkins the Thomist), that the 'book of life' may indeed have printed pages, has been made to seem mandarin. We can no longer simulate Dante's *moto spirituale* and physical dwelling inside the *Aeneid*, in the sensible construct of the *Summa* or next to Statius' *Thebaid*. We simply no longer read what Dante and the house of European intellect supposed to be the shared alphabet of reason and recognition. References, citations, implicit parallels which make up the constant texture of the *Commedia*, have to be looked up. This exercise, if one is at all conscientious about it, proves covertly destructive. The poem recedes as the footnotes thicken and grow more insistently elementary. The astringency and sheer speed of Dante's narrative, the lucid tautness which harries foward even clotted episodes of abstruse inquiry, are fatally lost. Second-handedness and stale academicism interpose.

Conditioned, moreover, by an aesthetic of the fragmentary, of the 'original', of the open-ended, we balk at the omnivorous authority, at the formal enclosedness of the *Commedia*. These reactions probably disable us in regard to the whole epic mode. We no longer turn with ease to 'long' poems. We have relegated to the display case that central axis of imaginative, intellectual and political summation which extends from Homer and Virgil to Milton, Klopstock and the Victor Hugo of the *Légende des siècles* and of those last, unread, stunning epics on God and Satan. We scarcely glance at the 'epics on the epic' produced by Boiardo, Ariosto and Tasso, though it is precisely this current which energizes much of English romantic literature and Byron in particular. Who, today, reads Camões's *Lusiads*, that bracing pageant of which *different* English translations were published in 1826, 1853, 1854, 1877, 1878 and 1880? It is the cunning genius of Pound's *Cantos* (in this respect so intimately heir to Browning's long poems) to quarry the epic convention while staying bitty, idiosyncratic, incomplete and radically egotistical in the modern anti-epic vein.

This slipping out of focus pertains also to the 'microscopic'. Consider the phases of the Pilgrim's leavetaking from Virgil towards the close of the *Purgatorio*.

At the end of Canto XXVII, Virgil defines the limits of his own ethical and intellectual apprehension. He now 'crowns' and 'mitres' Dante 'over yourself' — *te sovra te corono e mitrio* — an intricate turn of phrase pointing to the supreme degree of inner justice, or imperial discipline and self-governance to which Virgil, the pre-eminent Augustan, has conducted his charge. A scarcely accented nuance in line 4 of XXVIII tells us that Dante, for the very first time in the journey, takes the lead on his own. In line 56 of the following Canto, he who has almost invariably been titled *maestro* or *duca* is now only *buon Virgilio*. At the approach of Beatrice, 'clad in the hue of living flame', Dante turns one last time to his erstwhile mentor but refers to him simply as 'Virgil'. Yet never has the *Aeneid* itself been more radiantly present. 'I know the signs of the ancient ardour' says Dante as the veiled lady nears. He is quoting directly from Dido to Anna in Book IV, 23: *adgnosco veteris vestigia flammae*. Then comes the tercet of formal valediction which names Virgil thrice and bestows on him the final dignity of *dolcissimo patre*. This triple invocation belongs to two unifying sets: that of numerological balance (he is to be named one last time by Beatrice, giving us a deliberate 1+3+1 pattern), and that of classical precedent (the threefold appellation of Eurydice in Virgil's *Georgics* IV, 525-27, a poignant mirroring of an earlier loss and infernal descent). Thus we have echo inside echo and a *diminuendo* in which every interval is minutely controlled.

The craft required is one of sophisticated 'audition'. It demands not only extreme concentration but an ability to keep in mind, to maintain in sub-surface motion, the local detail while perceiving the design as a whole. However muted, it may be no more than a shift of tense or case, the present singularity must be kept in dynamic play against the major lineaments and elevations. The recognition of the submerged quote or pastiche, the grasp of contiguity and reciprocal qualification between moments in the text which may be far apart, must be quick and accurate but also unobtrusive, so as not to break the dominant pace.

The requisite habits of notation and pleasure are not arcane, merely obsolete. We have largely discarded the sense of poetry as a medium of natural universality. Functions of technical information, historical record, analytic argument, which are integral and obvious to Dante's use of verse are now almost completely a part of the 'prosaic'. We lack the silences (around, inside us), the deep-breathing fixity of total regard, without which that delicately resonant criss-cross of remembrance and shock on which the meaning of Virgil's going hinges cannot be heard. We inhabit noise-levels, bursts of static, stimuli of a kind which renders artificial, if not impossible, the necessary immersion in and self-gathering towards the jealous exigencies of Dante's text.

On a routine level: we no longer learn by heart and our textual memories are skin-deep. But in its organic recourse to previous poetry, to mythology, to topographical and chronological markers, it is on memory that Western high literature, and the epic especially, relies. Reading responsibly one not only spots the citation but, out of a trained, focused silence, speaks the next line. The exact retrieval of the Virgil invocations of XXVII and XXVIII is made, almost unconsciously, when we pick up the motif in Cantos XXIX and XXX. Musicians have active memory in their lips and fingers, over great runs and intricacies of material. So had the reader whom Dante intended, or Heidegger when reading Hölderlin and Trakl. But overall, the needed silences, literacies, inhibitions of distraction, acceptances of verse as a central public idiom, on all of which the current vitality of the *Commedia* depends, are either lapsed or, more grimly, restricted to the specialist. Thus there is in the largesse of Professor Singleton's presentation more than a hint of melancholy, of doubt as to those whom his labours might serve.

But there are inherent barriers as well. The *Divina Commedia* exhibits a tenacious streak of sadism. To be sure, times were ferocious. Counterfeiters, failed astrologers, mavericks of diverse persuasions were burnt alive. According to the edict banishment, Alighieri himself would have been if the authorities had snatched him on Florentine ground. Starvation, the vengeance of mercenaries and mobs on whole communities, individual refinements of terror were commonplace. Hence the monumental vehemence of petty ambush, street-brawl or family mayhem in the calendar of Tuscan life. But there is in Dante's complexion a more obscure, philosophical cruelty. He is a virtuoso of pain, as if to counterpoise the exceeding suavity and femininity of his love-poetry and *Vita Nuova*. He lingers over torment, and adds. Corso Donati's demise, as reported in Villani's history, is ugly enough. Forese's prophecy (*Purgatorio* XXIV, 82ff) embroiders. The detested captain of the exiled Neri faction is dragged to Hell at the tail of a horse, his body lashed about and hideously disfigured. Commentators have tried to give the passage an allegoric varnish; but it is unmistakably literal. It is Dante visiting chastisement on one whom he sees as a traitor. The loving specificities of torture in the *Inferno* are renowned. Medieval frescoes of after-life (at Torcello, in Siena, in the Umbrian churches), Church sermons, popular beliefs, abound in similar agonies. But again, it is the fine-nerved probing of Dante's art, the nobility of the performative idiom, which makes the effect blacker and more personal. The man's proud heart is in it.

Coming after the Nazi-Stalinist blood-sports, we are less ready to tune in with these sanctified bestialities. We sense today to what subterranean but cumulative extent the Christian teaching and vision of everlasting, sterile incarceration and punishment in Hell prefigured, perhaps made potentially real, the method of the concentration camps. There is something beside travesty in the Nazi proposition that the camps were merely 'Hell above ground'. Dante's is the loftiest part, yet a part none the less, of a long reverie on omnipotence and pain. Dreams can turn to habit.

At the other end, no amount of commentary pointing to concreteness, to dramatic tension, will make the *Paradiso* fully accessible. The tremolo is so long-sustained, the effulgence so unwavering, as to produce, however we take it, a banality of the sublime. The lobby-politics, visceral processes and artillery which Milton implants in Heaven are an attempt to liven what is, fundamentally, an intractable topic. Some element of real presence ebbs out of the *Commedia*, at least for the non-theologian, once the lady Matelda has wafted us over Lethe. We have, complains Eliot, 'a prejudice against beatitude as material for poetry'.

The trouble lies deeper. The verbal exchanges in Paradise are tautologies, harmonious reiterations of certitude. Living speech must have in it the shadow-side and roughage of possible duplicity. In Hell and Purgatory, Dante compels us to listen and read between the lines. In Paradise such wariness would be blasphemous. As perfect verity burns through it, the medium pales. There is, therefore, more than allegory to Dante's use of babytalk, as he approaches the rose of fire. We are out of line with the hymnal innocence, the cherubim, the low-content magnificats — poetical, plastic, orchestral — of the Victorians and Pre-Raphaelites. Eliot insisted that he had 'revolted' against Rossetti and, by inference, against Rossetti's version of Dante; but he was nearer to it than we.

Whatever the reasons, the fact is obvious. Dante is fairly well absent from the syllabus, from the currency of pleasure and implicitness which make a classic text ramify into daily feeling. He comes to us in snippets or at second hand. (Do Italians still read the *Commedia*?)

Yet we need not commit the heresy of viewing our own time as of singular, tragically-elect significance to notice that there is in the *Commedia* much that concerns us. Dante remains the master welder of poetry to politics. He conjoins the disinterested criteria of the literary and philosophic imagination to the partisan grit and myopia of political activism. He knows, he instructs us, that the claims of political constraint and manœuvre are, at the level of individual conscience, largely spurious; that violence makes systematic the inchoate tug of opportunism. Poetry must make shapeliness of politics if these are to be endured. But not past a certain point; otherwise a false comeliness will do as apologia for inhumanity and muddle. No other writer, not Dostoevsky or Conrad, though they come close, has matched Dante's simultaneous response to the opposed criteria of ideological elegance (the imperial paradigm, the ideal of civic *dignitas*) and of the technical, empirical actuality of power. To come down to 'relevance': it is in the *Commedia* that the logic of a European union has its best substance.

Another issue, sharply of our time, is that of the reach of language in respect of abstraction, particularly scientific. How far can non-specialised speech include, harness to general sensibility and personal judgment, the codes of the natural and applied sciences? Can the proliferating enormities – the term being one of dimension as well as of moral and psychological potential – of biology, physics, medicine, cosmology, be brought back, even if only via metaphor, into the vulgate? If no such repatriation is feasible, ordinary discourse will find itself ever more isolated from the new models of reality, from the new patterns of 'true' sense as they are expressed in the mathematical and formal dialects of the scientist. The sciences, in turn, will find themselves absurdly eccentric to the home ground of general cognisance. The early fourteenth-century condition was obviously less polarised than our own. But in its own terms, Dante's encompassing of the technical, extending from his sure grasp of the esoteric routines of tinker and tailor to his metaphoric 'packaging' of physiology, alchemy, astronomy, remains exemplary. No writer has surpassed him in incorporating and giving tactile authority to scientific metaphysical speculations. Reading the *Commedia* we learn of the several ways in which symbol, analogue, simile, metaphor and trope can translate abstruse knowledge and 'technicity' into common feeling. The challenge has nagged since Pope's adroit domestication of Newtonian celestial mechanics. Dante suggests that even the outermost reconnaissance of science or philosophic hypothesis can, must be retrieved for the human imagination, and that poetry is the natural voice of recall.

Homecoming is decisive. Glancing at the extravagant range of allusion and cosmological spaces in the *Commedia*, Péguy rounded on 'Dante, ce *globe-trotter*'. But the centre is in fact magnetic and reductive: *Toscana sonò tutta.* Thus nothing in the whole epic is more charged with meaning than the wrench of homesickness at the start of *Paradiso* XXV. In the middle of the blaze of transcendent felicity, the poet dreams of his return to the 'fair sheepfold'. All pastoral is an attempt to come home. This is why the choice of words in this supreme passage is so exact:

> del bello ovile ov' io dormi' agnello,
> nimico ai lupi che li danno guerra.
>
> (from the fair sheepfold where I slept as a lamb, an enemy to the wolves which war on it. . . .)

We have seen how even in nether Hell citizenships are minutely noted. A man is of this borough, shire, mountain-eyrie. The *Commedia* becomes a great spiral and peregrination of return. We are, just now, visibly dislocated. Our landscapes are cannibalized and ephemeral. Poetry tells of a man's 'housedness' in his past and self. It would find him at home in the skin of his speech and among the objects, organisms, terrains which circle his being. Poetry grafts boundlessness on to the familiar, irreducible branch. Dante's sole never leaves the ground (let the pun be). The *Divina Commedia* performs that mystery of rooted motion without which there is no public sense or private weight to our lives.

Either we yield to *la bufera infernale*, the sinister whirl-wind, or start heading for home. The dark wood is not a bad place in which to begin.

8

After the Book?

1972

It is like us to ask such questions. They are, in several ways, symptomatic of the present climate of feeling. We are ready to ask very large and inherently destructive questions. This is radicalism in a special sense. Not Hegelian-Marxist radicalism with its implicit futurity, with its almost axiomatic presumption that we go to the root of a problem in order to solve it, and because we know that destruction, uprooting, is only a necessary risk before solution. No; our going to the root of things is more ambivalent. We would do so even when we are not confident that there *is* a solution. It may be, in fact, that the aspect of demolition, the apocalyptic strain, gently tempt us. We are fascinated by 'last things', by the end of cultures, of ideologies, of art forms, of modes of sensibility. We are, certainly since Nietzsche and Spengler, 'terminalists'. Our view of history, says Lévi-Strauss in a deep pun, is not an anthropology but an 'entropology'.

This makes for intellectual exhilaration and a kind of bleak nobility. It is, presumably, not every species that can meditate its own ruin, not every society that can image its own decay and possible subjection to new and alien energies. But it is a negative radicalism which carries with it an element of self-fulfilment. This is a large, intricate topic. As I have tried to show elsewhere, a good deal of the political barbarism of the politics of our century was anticipated, dreamt of, fantasized about in the art, literature, and apocalyptic theories of the previous hundred years. It makes sense — although only in a dialectical way — to ask whether a force of prevision of the order of Kafka's does not in some manner

'Prepare', 'prepare for' the lunacies and inhumanities which it intimates. If we ask, therefore, whether there is a future for books or what may come after the end of books, we may be doing more than pose a question. The fact that we *can* and *do* ask may be part of the process of debilitation which, presumably, we fear; and it could, conceivably, hasten it. It is a famous saying of Marx that mankind does not ask major questions until there is the objective possibility of an answer. This may be so. But there is another, more disturbing way of putting it; mankind may only ask certain questions in order to elicit a negative, predictive reply.

Obviously, however, we are not asking in a spirit of indifferent inquiry or nihilistic play. If we pose the question of the viability of the book, it is because we find ourselves in a social, psychological, technical situation which gives this question substance. And although we hope to press the question home and to look scrupulously at the evidence, we hope also that the question will resolve itself positively; that our asking is, in Hegel's incisive terminology, an *Aufhebung*. Asking is an action, a possible bringing into view and into being of perspectives in which the question is seen to be trivial or falsely posed. Or, at the rare best, to ask is to provoke not the answer one actually fears or aims at, but the first contours of a new and better asking — which is then a first kind of answer. Bearing this in mind, let us sketch very briefly some of the historical and pragmatic grounds which make it possible and even responsible to envisage the end of the book as we have known it.

First, it is worth stressing that the 'book as we have known it' has been a significant phenomenon only in certain areas and cultures, and only during a relatively short span of history. Being bookmen we tend to forget the extremely special locale and circumstances of our addiction. We lack anything like a comprehensive history of reading. It would, I think, show that reading in our sense — 'with unmoving lips' — does not predate St.Augustine (who first remarked on it) by very much. But I would narrow the range even further. The existence of the book as a common, central fact of personal life depends on economic, material, educational preconditions which hardly predate the late sixteenth century in western Europe and in those regions of the earth under direct European influence. Montaigne and Bacon are already bookmen, and profoundly conscious of the relations of their own inner life to the future of the printed form. But even they read in a way which is not entirely ours; their sense of the authority, of the layered hermeticism of the written word — from surface level to anagogical mystery — has much in common with an earlier, almost pictorial or 'iconic' view of meaning. Our style of reading, the unforced currency of our business with books, is not easy to document before, say, Montesquieu. It climaxes in Mallarmé's well-known pronouncement that the true aim of the universe, of all vital impulse, is the creation of a supreme book — *le Livre*. Now the relevant time span is only about a century and a half. Yet it is undoubtedly true that Mallarmé himself marks the beginning of the questions we are asking here.

The classic age of the book depended on a number of material factors (even as we have no full history of reading, we have no sociology of reading, though there are in the criticism of Walter Benjamin and in Adorno's sociology of music numerous indications as to what is needed).

The book on the monastery lectern or in the chained university library is not the same as that of the seventeenth century. In its classic phase, the book is a privately owned object. This requires the conjunction of specific possibilities of production, marketing, and storage. The private library is far more than an architectural device. It concentrates a very complicated spectrum of social and psychological values. It requires and, in turn, determines certain allocations of space and silence which impinge on the house as a whole. In visual and tactile terms, it favours particular formats or genres — the two are intimately meshed — over others: say the bound volume over the pamphlet, the in-octavo over the folio, the *opera omnia* or set over the single title. The spiritual cannot be divorced from the physical fact. A man sitting alone in his personal library reading is at once the product and begetter of a particular social and moral order. It is a *bourgeois* order founded on certain hierarchies of literacy, of purchasing power, of leisure, and of caste. Elsewhere in the house there is most likely a domestic who dusts the shelves of books, who enters the library when called. And there are children schooled not to make undue noise, not to burst in when their father is reading. In short, the classic act of reading — what is depicted as *la lecture* in so many eighteenth-century genre paintings and engravings — is the focus of a number of implicit power relations between the educated and the menial, between the leisured and the exhausted, between space and crowding, between silence and noise, between the sexes and the generations (it is only very gradually that women come to read in the same way and context as their husbands, brothers, and fathers).

These power relations and value-assumptions have been drastically eroded. There are few libraries now in private apartments and fewer servants to dust them or oil the book spines. Intensities of light and noise levels of an unprecedented volume crowd in on personal space, particularly in the urban home. Far more often than not, the act of reading takes place against, in direct competition with another medium — television, radio, the record player. There are almost no taboo-spaces or sacrosanct hours left in the modern family. All is free zone. Where the book shelves were, we tend to find the record cabinet and the row of LPs (this, in itself, is one of the most important changes in the climate, in the enveloping matrix of our intellectual and emotional lives). It is only rarely in the home that the exercise of reading, in the old sense, now takes place. It is in highly specialized frameworks: mainly the university library or academic 'office'. We are almost back at the stage before Montaigne's famous circular reading room in the quiet tower. We read 'seriously' as did the clerics, in special professional places, where books are professional tools and silence is institutional.

The modern paperback is an immediate and brilliantly efficient embodiment of the new parameters. It take very little space. It is quasi-disposable. Its compactness declares that it can be, is almost intended to be, used 'in motion', under casual and fragmented circumstances. Being quite explicitly of the same material make-up as trash fiction, the paperback — even where its content is highbrow — proclaims an easy democracy of access. It carries with it no manifest sign of economic or cultural élitism. Mickey Spillane and Plato share the same book rack in the airport lounge or drug store.

But the mainsprings of change in the status of the book lie deeper. Definite philosophic beliefs and habits of perception underlay the primacy of the book in the life of the mind from the time of Descartes to that of Thomas Mann (one of the last complete representatives of the classic stance). Having tried to make some of these points in detail in previous work, I will do no more than summarize.

In very large measure, most books are about previous books. This is true at the level of the semantic code: writing persistently refers to previous writing. Explicit or implicit citation, allusion, reference are essential means of designation and proposition. It is via this dynamism of reiteration that the past has its most palpable existence. But the process of reference is even more comprehensive. Grammar, the literary idiom, a genre such as a sonnet or a prose novel, embody a previous formalization of human experience. Thoughts, feelings, events as set down in books do not come raw; the format of expression carries with it very strong and complex, though often 'subliminal', values and boundaries. In a suggestive essay, some years ago, E.H.Gombrich showed that even the most violent, spontaneous of pictorial notations — Goya's sketches of the insurrection in Madrid — are stylized by, filtered through, previous works of art. So it is with books: all literature has behind it human experience of the kind which previous literature has identified as meaningful. The act of writing for the printed page as it conjoins with the reading response is intensely 'axiomatized' or conventionalized, however fresh and turbulent the author's impulse. The past is strongly at his back; the current moves between bounds of established possibility.

These elements of tradition and limitation are of the essence of a classic world view. If Western literature — from Homer and Ovid to *Ulysses* and *Sweeney Among the Nightingales* — has been so largely referential, each major work mirroring what has gone before and bending the light only so much out of a given focus and no more, the reason lies at the very heart of our literacy. Western and Chinese culture have been bookish in a very definite way; Western culture unfolds, by highly self-conscious modes of imitation, variation, renascence, parody, or *pastiche*, from a strikingly small set of canonic, classical texts and form-models, principally Greek. By creative 'ingestion', as Ben Jonson put it, the curve of discourse tends from Homer to Virgil, from Virgil to Dante, from Dante to Milton, Klopstock, Joyce, and the explicit retrospective of the *Cantos*. There have been fifteen *Oresteias* and a dozen *Antigones* in twentieth-century drama and opera. Archilochus points to Horace, Horace to Jonson, Jonson to Dryden and Landor, Landor to Robert Graves. The line, the experience of lament over the poet or hero who has died young is unbroken since the *Greek Anthology* and passes, via stages of massive cross-reference, through *Lycidas* and *Adonais* to Arnold's *Thyrsis*, Tennyson's *In Memoriam*, and Auden's elegy — built of Ovidian echoes — on the passing of Yeats. Print and the physique of books have been the enforcing framework of tradition. It is in this respect — not in any vague, undemonstrable intimation of visual-linear compulsion — that we can characterize Western culture as being that of the library at Alexandria, of Gutenberg and of Caxton.

This close correlation of formal invention, of energized feeling with established genres and a framework of allusion and prepared echo has further implications. *Le Livre* is the proven talisman against death. This is the grand discovery, the proud cry, in Homer and Pindar. The words of the poet outlive the events they narrate and make the poet immortal. Rephrased by Horace and by Ovid the promise that time cannot gnaw great words to dust, that they will outlast the brass and marble on which they are incised, is the password of Western literature. 'I die, my life may have been a shamble of error and non-recognition, but if my book has truth and beauty enough, it will endure. There are those as yet unborn who shall read it, as I read the classic on my table.' This is the secret of Demodocus, the minstrel in the *Odyssey*, and, two and a half millennia later, of Paul Éluard when he states *le dur désir de durer*.

The gamble on immortality can only come off if language itself holds. There is nothing mystical about this notion. It is a traditional trope of Western literature, particularly poetry, that words are inadequate to the needs of personal expression, that available language falls drastically short of the poet's inner vision. But this trope is itself linguistically articulated. The anguish of unattainable precision or radiance is real enough, but it is also conventional and is itself a means of eloquence. The Petrarchan sonnet springs constantly and with confident elaboration from a basic complaint about its own insufficiency to state the uniqueness, the vehemence of the poet's love. Mystical writings, such as the *Canciones* of St.John of the Cross come nearest the limit; but we know this just because they communicate to us in words of great precision and clarity their sense of the neighbourhood of the inexpressible.

Here again, the complex of the book and of its reader stands in a specific Judaic-Hellenic descent. It is from these two antique sources, so oddly, so intensely literary and bookish in their self-definition, that we derive our view of the eminent worth and stability of speech. These two civilizations tell us that the word — the *logos* — is central to man's religion, to his *log*ic, to his mytho*log*ies. They tell us that the relations of descriptive adequacy between human language and the 'outside world' may be epistemologically opaque, that there are deep problems about meaning what we say and saying what we mean, about understanding one another and about denoting objects or sense-data unambiguously. None the less, this very opaqueness can only be diagnosed and registered in words, linguistically. We inhabit a language-world, and if it is the source of perplexing but marginal dilemmas, it is also the root of our conscious being and mastery over nature.

This conviction, of which books are the active incarnation, prevails with only eccentric challenges from the time of the great oral epics at least to that of Rimbaud and Surrealism.

Each of these philosophic tenets and the psychological attitudes which accompany them have come under severe attack. (Perhaps one ought to have realized earlier how fragile the fabric of Western literacy was, how delicate and probably unique were the historical, moral raw materials which went into its making.)

The basis of referential recognition on which our poetry and prose have operated from Chaucer to T.S.Eliot, from the *Roman de la rose* to Valéry, has become the increasingly fictive possession of a mandarin few. The organized amnesia of American schooling — and much of Europe is following suit — ensures that the alphabet of scriptural, mythological, historical allusion in our literature has become a hieroglyph. Footnotes lengthen on the page as rudimentary identifications and paraphrase are needed. Off balance on top of these explanatory stilts, the poem itself becomes strange and blurred. More and more of our verbal inheritance is caught between the semi-literacy of the mass market and the Byzantine minutiae of the specialist. In the glass case of the academic storehouse verse, drama, fiction which was once a common presence now leads an immaculate but factitious life. Authority — and authority is the core, the wellspring of formal tradition — is itself highly suspect. Ezra Pound's 'make it new' was, in fact, a call for renovation in the Renaissance sense. The cry of the new millenarians against the classic, against eloquence, against that which is difficult of access, is something entirely different. It goes back to the terrorist insight of Dada that the literate past must be destroyed, dynamited, if history is to enter a phase of radical innocence.

The aim of survival, of glory in the pantheon, is equally suspect. It speaks of hierarchy and academicism. We seem to be involved in a revolution of time-values. *Now* is everything, and the young regard as hypocrisy, opportunism, or worse, the traditional strategy of the poet or thinker sacrificing his present life to future eminence. This equivocation, self-evident to Milton, to Keats, to Hölderlin, now has a ring of hollow bathos. To the radical generation there is obscenity in Mallarmé's belief that a supreme masterpiece, *le Livre*, is the goal and validation of human affairs. Today Pisarev's slogan, 'a pair of boots outweighs Shakespeare and Pushkin', has come into its own.

The doubts about language have more varied and respectable sources. Again, I have dealt with this theme at length previously and will only summarize here. In the period from Rimbaud and Mallarmé to Dada and Surrealism an 'anti-language' movement springs up from inside literature. Bored by the oppressive eloquence and perfections of the past, the new iconoclasts and experimenters sought to recreate the word, to find in new verbal and syntactic forms intact resources of exactitude, of magic, of sub-conscious energy. The Dada demand for 'an end to the word' is at once nihilistic — man cannot be renewed if he keeps his worn skin of speech — and aesthetic. It calls for the discovery of hitherto unexploited phonetic, iconic, and semiological means. A second current of doubt is that which stems from formal logic and the work of logical positivism and of Wittgenstein. It is one of the major effects of modern philosophy, from Moore to Austin and Quine, to have made language look messier, more fragile, less comfortably concordant with our needs, than before. The confidence in the medium which animates earlier philosophic monuments — those of Kant, of Hegel, of Schopenhauer, of Bergson — is simply no longer available. A third impulse to linguistic scepticism comes from the enormous expansion of the exact sciences. An ever-increasing portion of sensory and conceptual reality has passed into the keeping of the non-verbal semantic systems of mathematics. A modern writer can deal precisely, and in the relevant idiom, with far less of natural fact and intellectual analysis than could Shakespeare, Milton, or Pope. The fourth aspect is that first investigated by Karl Kraus and George Orwell:

the cheapening, the dehumanization, the muddling of words through the mass media and through the lies of barbarism in modern politics. This brutalization and profanation of the word is very probably one of the main causes for the tide of self-destruction, either through self-imposed silence or actual suicide, which has come over Western literature from the time of Nerval and Rimbaud to that of Sylvia Plath, Paul Celan, and John Berryman. The words in my mouth, says Ionesco, have gone dead.

Taken together, these attacks on traditional literacy, on the transcendental view of the artist's and thinker's enterprise, and on the validity of language, constitute a fundamental critique of the book. It is not so much a 'counter-culture' which is being developed, but an 'after-culture'.

But once we have made this analysis, the factual question arises: *are* people reading less, is there an empirically demonstrable decline in the vitality of printed books?

The evidence is very difficult to come by. Robert Escarpit's *La Révolution du livre* (1966) is the only full-scale study I known of, and it is, at best, preliminary. What we find are fragments of information, isolated statistics, guesses of every kind.

A survey conducted in 1970 indicates that on average a French man or woman will read no more than *one* book a year. The figure for Italy is thought to be even less as there are extensive pockets of sub-literacy. In Germany, on the other hand, the ratio is rather better. The number of book-stores in the United States — i.e., of stores primarily or exclusively devoted to the sale of serious books and able to keep a representative selection in stock — has diminished drastically over the past twenty years (I have heard the figure of closures of 'hybridizations' put as high as 50 per cent). The turnover rate has accelerated formidably, especially in regard to fiction. If it is not immediately successful, a new novel will remain only very briefly in the bookstore. The ratio of remaindered prose fiction to what is kept in stock from among the estimated thirty or forty novels published weekly in the English language is, obviously, dramatic. The economics of serious hardcover publishing have become fairly lunatic. Prices have trebled and often quadrupled between successive volumes in the same set or series. In numerous cases publication would not be feasible at all were it not for complex, often hidden schemes of subsidization or for immediate tie-ups with the paperback market. It is, currently, no more than a sober platitude that the whole future of the commercial production and distribution of hardcover books with only a limited circulation is in doubt. The wild circus of personnel changes among American publishing houses, the spate of takeovers, the febrile vulgarization of once-great lists, are only the external symptom of a deep malaise in the whole book-world.

To these facts I would add one or two personal observations, obviously subjective and very limited in scope. Paperbacks do *not* make for the collection of a library. Among the very many students I have met and taught in several countries over the past two decades, fewer and fewer are book-collectors, fewer and fewer reject the prepackaged selectivity of the paperback in order to own *complete* works of an author. Among these same young people there appears to be a marked decline in habits of solitary, exclusive reading. They know less and less of literature *by heart*. They read against a musical background or in company. Almost instinctively, they resent the solipsism, the egotistical claims on space and silence implicit in the classic act of reading. They wish to shut no one out from the empathic tide of their consciousness. Being something we can listen to personally yet share fully with others at the same moment and in the same place, music, far more than books, meets the present ideal of participatory response. It is not the 'dog-eared volume' we find in the walker's pocket, but the transistor. And because it allows access at so many level — ranging from technical insight to the vague wash of semi-conscious echo — music allows that democracy of emotion which literature, particularly difficult literature, denies. In brief: so far as I can make out, the prime requisites of concentrated reading in the old sense — aloneness, silence, contextual recognitions — are growing rare in the very milieu in which we would most crucially look for them — that of the undergraduate.

These are, I repeat, *ad hoc* and piecemeal impressions. They are nearly impossible to quantify. We are too close to these new tendencies and problems to have more than a very indistinct view. My observations would, I suspect, not be true of the Soviet Union, which is in a phase of centrally determined, almost Victorian literacy. They are only partly true of those countries of eastern Europe in which reading is often the best way of showing opposition to the regime, and in which competing electronic media remain underdeveloped. Nevertheless, and with regard to our own setting, I would say that the world of the bookman is much diminished.

Hence one's readiness to speculate — it can be no more than that — on what may come after the book or what may happen to books in a period of cultural transition.

It is now a commonplace that audio-visual means of communication are taking over wide areas of information, persuasion, entertainment, which were, formerly, the domain of print. At a time of global increase in semi- or rudimentary literacy (true literacy is, as I have tried to suggest, in fact, decreasing), it is very probable that audio-visual 'cultural packages', i.e. in the guise of casettes, will play a crucial role. It is already, I think, fair to say that a major portion of print, as it is emitted daily, is, at least in the broad sense of the term, a caption. It accompanies, it surrounds, it draws attention to material which is essentially pictorial. When uttered on the radio and, to a far greater degree, when spoken on television, language has a specialized, perhaps ancillary status. The phenomenon can be exaggerated; contrary to McLuhan's expectations, radio is holding its own, particularly in such hyper-verbal genres as discussion or drama. It is none the less obvious that a great part of humanity now receives its main informational and evocative stimuli in the form of images and illustrative signal-codes. The astonishing fact is not that this should be so, but that the word in the old sense should still be so vital. We touch here on an extremely puzzling phenomenon. Even the most superb of movies can only be seen a very limited number of times (say five or six) before it goes stale, before an impression of utter inertness takes over. Why should this be? In what way is a piece of print — a poem, a chapter in a novel, a scene from a play — any less 'fixed', static, unchanging than a film frame? Yet we can read the same poem a hundred times over in our lives and it will literally be new to us. Where does the difference lie? What is there about purely visual material which does not have the inherent repeatability, the sameness within change which is the attribute of the written word? So far as I know, neither aesthetics nor psychology have come up with an answer. But the evidence is, I believe, unmistakable, and it entails a power of survival for printed speech which no competing medium has.

The more radical, though less visible changes, are those occurring not in the communication of material but in its storage and analytic treatment. Information storage and retrieval by means of data banks and computers are far more than technical devices. They constitute little less than a new way of organizing human knowledge and the relations of present inquiry to past work. All taxonomies are, in essence, philosophical. Any library system, whether by size or Dewey, enacts a formalized vision of how the world is put together, of what are the optimal sight-lines between the human mind and phenomenological totality. Electronic indexing and memorization, the instant provision of information according to various grids and semantic markers, will profoundly alter not only the physical structure of libraries, but our proceedings in them. The key concepts of referential relevance and of context (the books further down the shelf, the ones we needed most but did not know we were looking for) will change. Data banks are not for browsing. In many disciplines, moreover, the cut-off point of chronological utility will be codified and institutionalized. One will not be expected to cite, to be aware of, material earlier than a very recent point on the index tape. It will thus become ever more difficult to resist the illusion — and it *is* an illusion, certainly so far as most humanities go — that insight is cumulative, that there is a necessary progress and teleology in the statement of feelings and ideas. The 'programming' of knowledge in the electronically-managed libraries of the future will, I think, bring on alterations of sensibility, modifications in our habits of discovery, as significant as any since the invention of moveable type. The formula is one that makes for the minimalization of hazard, of waste, of spill-over. Yet it is these counter-utilitarian aspects of traditional reading which have determined much of the best in our culture.

What of the more immediate prospects for the printed book? It is perhaps foolhardy to conjecture. But some lines of change are already clear. There may be fewer serious books published. The current rate of over-production, notably in fiction, has triggered an absurd, ultimately self-defeating spiral of small printings, mounting overheads and inability to amortize costs at anything near the rate regarded as indispensable in other industries. There may be fewer publishers, and it looks as if the edition and production of books, particularly in America, is passing into the hands of a small number of large consortia, often allied with, financed by, other industries or capital holdings. What seems to be emerging is a pattern of giants together with a few small, specialized houses whose actual structure resembles that of the 'little magazine' in relation to the mass media. The search for a technological break-through in regard to production costs will intensify. The restrictive and inflationary practices in the printing trades plainly reflect a luddite, terminal mood. The industry feels that its days are numbered. Whether some radical new photoprocess will emerge, whether the electric typewriter points the way, is uncertain. But increasingly, the hard-cover book printed (let alone illustrated) by traditional manual-mechanical means, is an anachronism. It is viable only in very large editions, which are of course limited to a small percentage of the annual list.

Even more significantly, there will, I expect, be a frank polarization in our understanding of books and of what is meant by *reading*. A firmer distinction than has been current hitherto will emerge as between the immense iceberg bulk of semi-attentive reading — ranging from the advertisement billboard to the pulp novel — and genuine 'full' reading. The latter will, more and more, become the craft and pursuit of a minority trained to do the job and who themselves probably hope to write a book. It is precisely the disaster of mass education in the United States, but also in other overdeveloped consumer technocracies, to have blurred this vital difference. A large majority of those who passed through the primary and secondary school system can 'read' but not *read*. Theirs is a pseudo-literacy. Various measurements are possible. It has been estimated that the vocabulary and grammatical comprehension possessed by a considerable majority of American adults has stabilized around the age level of twelve or thirteen. An estimated 30 per cent of adult readers find it difficult to apprehend a dependent clause (a fact long familiar to the copy editors of advertisement agencies, magazines, trash fiction, and federal or state regulations). Because it is no longer a natural, immediate part of our schooling, reading in the full sense of referential recognition, of grammatical confidence, of focused attention will have to be taught as a particular art. Anyone who has tried to teach literature or history or philosophy to the average high school graduate will testify that this is what the task is all about. It can well be argued that reading in the full sense was always the prerogative of an élite, that our pictures of a lost literacy are idealized and never applied to more than an educated minority. But this does not inform the case. That minority held the centres of power and of example; its criteria were those of the culture as a whole. This is no longer true. It is far more honest and far more productive to admit that the standards and ideals of a full literacy are not self-evident, that they are not applicable to the majority in a populist society, that they represent a special skill. We do not, after all, demand that all citizens be trapeze artists. What we must try to see to, is that those who *want* to learn to read fully can do so and that they be allowed the critical space and freedom from competing noise in which to practise their passion. In our fantastically noisy, distracted milieu this minimal room for private response is not easily come by.

These guesses and provisional suggestions may seem pessimistic. They are not meant to be. There is a strong element of health in our diminutions. Too much has been printed; too much made glossily available. Lincoln or Carlyle tramping miles to read and to excerpt a book, provide an image to think about; as does Edwin Muir, new from the world of the crofters, chancing at an Edinburgh bookstall on the worn copy of *Zarathustra* which was to transform his inner and outer life. Because it has been made so easy, our sense of the act of reading has often grown facile. At the very outset of the centuries of high literacy, Erasmus tells of stooping in a muddy way to snatch up a torn piece of print, and of his cry of wonder and good fortune at the event. Tomorrow's bookmen may, perhaps, find themselves in a like condition. This might not be, altogether, a bad thing.

Index of proper names

Compiled by Patricia Utechin